I WANT TO DO SOMETHING ELSE

BUT I'M NOT SURE WHAT IT IS

Ron and Caryl Krannich, Ph.Ds

IMPACT PUBLICATIONS
Manassas Park, VA

ISBN: 1-57023-216-4

Library of Congress: 20041115607

Publisher: For information on Impact Publications, including current and forthcoming publications, authors, press kits, online bookstore, and submission requirements, visit the left navigation bar on the home page of our main company website: www.impactpublications.com.

Publicity/Rights: For information on publicity, author interviews, and subsidiary rights, contact the Media Relations Department: Tel. 703-361-7300, Fax 703-335-9486, or email: info@impactpublications.com.

Sales/Distribution: All bookstore sales are handled through Impact's trade distributor: National Book Network, 15200 NBN Way, Blue Ridge Summit, PA 17214, Tel. 1-800-462-6420. All special sales and distribution inquiries should be directed to the publisher: Sales Department, IMPACT PUBLICATIONS, 9104 Manassas Drive, Suite N, Manassas Park, VA 20111-5211, Tel. 703-361-7300, Fax 703-335-9486, or email: info@impactpublications.com.

Contents

1

Is There More to Life
Than This?

I T'S 7AM ON MONDAY MORNING. You've traveled this road
many times before. You had a great weekend with your family and
friends. Now you face another stressful one-hour drive to work
through heavy stop-and-go traffic. You tune into your favorite
morning drive talk show, which helps exercise your mind and keep you
current on the day's news and controversies. It's entertaining and infor-
mative talk that doesn't quite brighten what is otherwise a relatively
boring morning commute.

It's a Routine, Okay Job

You arrive at work, get a cup of coffee, force a smile, engage in small talk
with co-workers, go to your desk, and spend the rest of the day making
phone calls, meeting with people, putting out a few fires, and writing
reports. At 5 or 6pm you head for home in the midst of stop-and-go
traffic – more stress for you to endure. The rest of your workweek follows
a similar pattern. This is not exactly what you envisioned your work life
would be when you left school, but it pays the bills.

Restless Years, Wanderlust "What If" Dreams

Everyone thinks you're successful, but you're increasingly restless. This routine has gone on since you started with this company. You don't hate this job, but neither do you love it. Perhaps it's time for a change. It's hard to explain your exact feelings. You fell into this job by accident. In fact, much of your work life seems to be a result of haphazard events. You met a friend at an alumni gathering who recommended that you contact his boss about a job with this relatively prestigious firm. You made the phone call, sent a resume, and met with the company. After five grueling interviews, you felt you were lucky to be offered this job. Indeed, many people would love to be in your position!

It's an okay job. After all, it's steady work that gives you a decent paycheck that is more than enough to pay the mortgage and live a comfortable lifestyle. The company is still standing in spite of the many mergers, downsizings, and outsourcings that have taken place in this industry recently. In fact, you often feel fortunate in having this job. You know you're better off than many of your friends. You like the people you work with, but your work isn't particularly challenging, and you often have difficulty keeping

> *Life is often a series of serendipitous events relived as a set of logical decisions that make perfect sense.*

motivated, enthusiastic, and focused. You have more interests and talents than those required by this job. It just doesn't seem like a good fit for you. You're ostensibly successful, but you're not really happy.

Your mind often wanders to personal and professional matters. You muse about greener pastures had you made other decisions at certain points in your life. Indeed, you sometimes talk to yourself about various "what if" career scenarios –

- what if you had gone to law school
- what if you had taken that job in Seattle
- what if you had not taken that first job
- what if you had attended University A rather than University B
- what if you had majored in chemistry rather than finance
- what if you had started a business rather than worked for others

- what if you had joined the Peace Corps rather than the Army
- what if you had stayed single rather than gotten married
- what if you hadn't been fired from your first job

At the same time, you often worry about your future. You know there are no guarantees in life, especially when it comes to a job or career these days. The job you have today may disappear tomorrow due to an economic downturn, bad business decisions, or outsourcing and offshoring to less expensive labor markets. If you've recently entered the job market, you may be looking for employment soon. If you are an older worker, at your age and level of experience, you know you are an endangered species. Given your salary and health benefits, you cost an employer lots of money, a cost he or she could cut significantly by hiring someone younger, with less experience, and perhaps with more current and fashionable skills. Despite what all the positive thinkers preach about taking charge of your life, you're not free to do whatever you would like to do. Doing what you love is often constrained by your educational level and the realities of economics, the job market, and your location.

You especially look forward to weekends. It's the time you can relax with family and pursue hobbies – photography, music, and gardening.

Finding Your Passion

You often think there must be more to life than what you're doing. Let's face it. You're good at what you do, but you simply don't have the passion for continuing this type of work. In fact, you often think about what really turns you on, such as photography. You know it's not your current job. Recently you've been thinking about this a lot. There has always been an element of wanderlust throughout your career – you have dreams about what you could have done better. You often end up doing things you really don't enjoy doing – but they are part of the job. But maybe it's not good to think or dream too much about your work. That's risky thinking. After all, you have a family to support and a mortgage to pay. Also, the job market is tough these days, and you're not sure what you would do if you lost this job.

You dread the thought of having to write a resume, network with strangers, and interview for another job. You're shy and not particularly entrepreneurial when it comes to looking for a job. In fact, you're probably lucky to have an ostensibly good job. If all goes well, you'll be able to retire in several years. However, your job could be offshored or the company could merge or go out of business. Perhaps you can pursue a second career after you retire, maybe one you missed out on when your life took this unexpected path.

Serendipitous Jobs, Accidental Careers

Despite all the talk about planning one's career and pursuing a passion, most people fall into jobs and careers by accident or happenstance: a part-time job that became permanent; a college research project that led to important job contacts; a casual conversation with a friend that turned into a job interview and offer; a life-changing vacation that led to a career change; a chance meeting with a recruiter; an enthralling hobby that became a job. Life is often a series of serendipitous events relived as a set of logical decisions that make perfect sense to the storytellers. They follow familiar paths rather than chart new directions based on a well-conceived plan. Perhaps they took a part-time job that turned into a long-term career. Or they talked to a friend who recommended that they apply for a particular job. They responded to a classified ad and landed a job. They left the military and took the first job that came along without knowing what they really wanted to do. After a few years of boredom and burnout, they think about changing jobs or careers. While they know what they **don't** want to do, which relates to their present job, they don't know what they **really** want to do next. They want to do something else with their career and life, but they don't know what it is.

What to Do With the Rest of Your Life

Each year millions of individuals face a similar restless issue that questions their current job satisfaction and points to a possible job or career change – *"I want to do something else, but I'm not sure what it is."* They feel it may be time to leave whatever they are doing, but they are uncertain about what they really want to do next in their life. Some see the signs and struggle with the fateful decision to make a job or career change by trying to formulate mission statements and career objectives and then develop a detailed plan of action – a job search – for realizing their dreams. Others know what they don't want to do, which is their current job, and proceed to write a weak resume that often communicates the wrong message to potential employers – they don't know what they really want to do. And still others stay around too long and thus have such decisions made for them – they lose their job for a variety of reasons.

If you've ever raised this issue, you're not alone. Most people know what they don't want to do, but they have difficulty articulating exactly what they want to do. Knowing when to stay and when to go is tied up with the notion of knowing what you want to do next with your life. If you could answer that question, you would know when it's time to go.

Quit Your Job and Grow Some Hair

Jobs or careers should not be life sentences. You should have the freedom to choose what you want to do, where you want to work, and with whom you want to associate. After all, we live in a highly mobile and opportunity-rich society where we have many job and career choices and where individuals are expected to have multiple careers and many jobs throughout their work life. In other words, we are supposed to have unlimited opportunities, if we make smart choices. But making critical job and career changes is always easier said than done. We could give you many examples of free-willed workers who made important life-changing career decisions. They quit their jobs to pursue other interests as well as changed careers.

> _Jobs or careers should not be life sentences. You should have the freedom to choose what you want to do, where you want to work, and with whom you want to associate._

But let's look at one instructive case that is both personal and well documented for cues on how to best answer our original question.

Gary was a very successful university professor and administrator who decided to quit his rather envious vice president job in order to pursue important community interests in the nonprofit sector (see his instructive story in Gary N. Rubin, **Quit Your Job and Grow Some Hair**, Impact Publications). Not surprisingly, he excelled in his new-found leadership position, which involved using his many community organization, fund-raising, and conflict resolution skills. He had the perfect personality for this highly interpersonal and increasingly political job. Socially adept and a seemingly natural networker, he handled most people and situations with extreme ease; everyone seemed to love Gary, even those who might disagree with him. However, after over 15 years in this once new and now tired career, he knew it was time to go. A very intuitive person, he perceived the signs everywhere. The job had become more and more political and stressful, and the personal and professional rewards were no longer evident nor forthcoming. While he knew he didn't want to continue in this job, he wasn't sure exactly what he really wanted to do next with his life. He and his wife were very much involved with the community where they lived, and he had a family to support, including a daughter who was about to enter college. Quitting this job would most likely mean uprooting the family, leaving the community, and taking a salary cut. Not many people voluntarily leave a high-level executive position with such a prestigious nonprofit organization. Indeed, some people might think he was crazy to make such a change. After all, those who do leave such jobs usually get fired or are lured away by more attractive offers from other organizations. He just needed to do something else with his life, but he wasn't sure what it was.

Gary approached this issue the way he usually approached his job and personal life – he decided to achieve greater clarity by networking with friends and professional acquaintances. He regarded this career change as an important introspective process – something that needed to be worked out by talking with many people about jobs, careers, interests, skills, and accomplishments. He contacted numerous friends and professional acquaintances, some of whom he had not spoken with for more than 20 years. He asked lots of questions and let everyone involved know he was "available" for employment that would best fit his interests and skills. The more he talked with others about his impending career change, the more he learned about himself and what he really wanted to do. This was not something he could get from reading books, taking self-assessment tests, or consulting with a career expert. He simply had to talk it through with his colleagues, peers, and potential employers. At the same time, members of his increasingly expanded network were well aware that he was in the job market looking for employment.

Similar to the conduct of research, this career change process would take a few months of serious thinking based on an active networking campaign. He would learn a great deal about himself and others – what he did and did not want to do and what others were looking for in today's job market. But he had to go through this exploratory process in order to clarify and specify his interests and goals as well as make critical job search connections. Once he reached a certain level of confirmed redundancy, he would know it was time to make the change. He knew he could always find another job, but at this stage in his life he wanted to find a job he really loved. While money was important, what he most valued were his family and friends. Finding a job that enabled him to fully use his skills and pursue important professional interests, minus the stress, was what he was really seeking.

While it seemed like a messy process, unplanned and serendipitous, within three months it worked well for Gary. Indeed, returning to his previous career, he landed a position as vice president with a university that fully utilized his community-based, fund-raising skills minus the intense stress of politics, at least for the moment. While university politics are ubiquitous and can be stressful, they are usually for low stakes and relatively manageable, especially when you are well positioned at the top.

For now, Gary has transitioned to the perfect job. He took the risk of exploring a new job and he approached the process right – through networking and research. After two years of reporting less stress and greater job satisfaction, he even says he has grown more hair!

Where Do You Go From Here?

The following pages are designed to assist you in answering one of the most important questions facing millions of individuals each year – What should I do next with my life? Through a series of principles, exercises, and stories, we outline a variety of approaches for dealing with this life-changing issue: *I want to do something else, but I'm not sure what it is.* What we reveal in the remainder of this book is nothing new or magical. The approaches have been used successfully by many individuals who regularly make job and career changes. We're not wedded to any one particular approach, only those that work for you. For what you will quickly see are a variety of bewildering approaches that claim success, from primarily understanding your personality type to seeking divine inspiration and intervention. What we try to do is bring a great deal of clarity to this issue by cutting through the many different approaches, questionable assumptions, and instant magic in the process of identifying strategies that will most likely work for you. In so doing, we pull together the most useful approaches for making critical job and career decisions.

Whatever you do, make sure you address the next stage in your work life with both a probing and positive attitude followed by specific actions rather than just reflection and wishful thinking. Take a proactive stance by raising lots of questions, taking tests, talking with influential people, and networking for information, advice, and referrals. This may initially seem to be a rather disorganized and messy planning process, but it will work for you in the end. As you will quickly discover, there is no substitute for taking purposeful action that both educates and connects you to individuals who can make a difference in your life. It takes time and patience as well as a good plan of action. Chances are your next job will come to you through a series of serendipitous events or lucky occurrences. That's the way it often happens. After all, you can plan your good luck by being in many different places with many different people who know you are actively seeking a job or career change. We're here to help you through this rather chaotic and serendipitous process.

> *There is no substitute for taking purposeful action that both educates and connects you to individuals who can make a difference in your life.*

2

Clarifying a Bewildering World of Approaches

DISCOVERING WHAT YOU want to do is by no means an easy task. Like many others who specialize in the art of counseling, including some pop psychologists, we could preach to you about the virtues of self-honesty, goal setting, positive thinking, planning, faith, and persistence. But chances are you would achieve a temporary psychological high, followed by a crash, attendant when such approaches encounter the realities of individual capabilities and implementation. Alternatively, while it would be nice to just take a pencil-and-paper, computerized, or online test that quickly reveals what you should do in the future, we've found no such magic bullets to give you reliable answers to important questions about your future. Short of seeing a fortune teller, this discovery process will take a combination of time, effort, and good luck.

Our Challenge

At best, we can suggest different strategies that will more or less help you discover what you do well and enjoy doing – the keys to clarifying that "something else" you might excel at in the future. Indeed, that's our mission throughout this book – bringing greater clarity to a subject that is often bewildering and frustrating to individuals who seek quick answers to where they may be going in the future. As you achieve such clarity, you will be in a much better position to make important career and life decisions.

The Future Is Now

The future is something we all would like to get a handle on to better predict and control. Knowing where we are heading in the next five years would simplify our lives considerably. Some people are very good at shaping their future through a combination of vision, planning, persistence, connections, and good luck. Other people, buffeted by forces beyond their control, live less predictable lives as they go with the flow of events. Elsewhere (***Change Your Job, Change Your Life***, page 8) we refer to these individuals as the "Great Getters" who are well advised to reassess their approach to life:

> They get an education; they get married and get a family; they get a house; they get a job; they get taxed; and they get buried. If they are lucky – as Andy Warhol would have us remember – they may even get famous for 15 minutes sometime during their lives. While they may plan for some major events in their lives, few people consciously shape their future through deliberate action on an ongoing basis.
>
> A career is something you **can** shape if you plan properly and have the requisite motivation and skills and use effective strategies to make it happen. However, the popular notion that all you need to do is get a good education that will lead to a good job and career, after which you live happily ever after, has been eroded in a society that has undergone rapid changes in education, training, occupations, and the workplace. The *"one job, one career, one work life"* phenomenon has all but ended for most occupations. The *"15 jobs, 5 careers, 10 geographic moves, and many work lives"* trend is now upon us in a new careering and re-careering era. As such, the future becomes synonymous with change. Therefore, you are well advised to anticipate, plan, and manage changes to your advantage.
>
> Without an analysis of your present, a vision of the future, and a plan of action, your future will most likely be a repeat performance of your past patterns of behavior. You will be blown by the winds of change and whims of chance rather than direct and control your own destiny.

As you will see throughout this book, understanding and transcending our past patterns of behavior are the keys to shaping our future. Once you discover who you are in terms of your pattern of motivations, interests, skills, values, accomplishments, and goals, a whole new world of decision-making will unfold before you. You will have a clear understanding of yourself and where you want to go in the future. Best of all, you'll know what else you'll want to do with your life!

> *Understanding and transcending our past patterns of behavior are the keys to shaping our future.*

Asking the Right Questions

Finding answers to important questions often lie in the quality of the questions we ask. Indeed, self-knowledge affecting decisions often begins with a set of questions that trigger important insights about ourselves. You should start by asking these questions:

1. What do I like and dislike about my current job?

2. What do I most value in work – money, working environment, colleagues, clients, nature of work, responsibilities, position, power, sense of accomplishment?

3. What things do I especially do well?

4. What things do I most enjoy doing?

5. What things would I like to do that I'm not doing at present?

6. If I had to start over with my education and training, what would I most prefer to study and be skilled in doing?

7. If I could design my perfect dream job, what would it look like in terms of skills, responsibilities, work settings, and the people I work with?

8. Where do I see my career going over the next 10 years?

9. How happy am I with my personal and professional lives?

10. If I could change any three things in my life – personal or professional – what would they be?

In the process of completing this book, you'll discover important answers to these questions that will help you chart a clear course of action in the coming months and years.

Learning Who You Are and Where to Go

The most important information you need for determining what you want to do focuses on you. While, as we will see in Chapter 5, it's important to know about alternative jobs and careers, and dream about things you might like to do, in the end you must first acquire as much information about yourself as possible – your values, interests, skills, abilities, temperament, and motivations – **before** deciding what you really want to do.

Ironically, most of us are more knowledgeable about our jobs and other people than about ourselves. For example, you may find it's far easier to talk about your job duties and responsibilities as well as the strengths and weaknesses of your bosses, co-workers, relatives, and friends than about your own strengths, weaknesses, and accomplishments. Being other-directed, we seldom take time to look within ourselves to discover who we really are and what we want to do beyond superficial notions of success. For example, have you formulated a personal mission statement or clarified your purpose in life? Doing so will give renewed meaning and significance to your life as well as help you focus on those things that really matter to you. Such an exercise also will give you direction and help you develop a job and career objective. As we will see in Chapter 9, the seemingly simple task of developing a 25-word objective can take a great deal of time since it requires you to seriously reflect on your past, present, and future.

As you will quickly discover, there are several approaches for acquiring career-related information on yourself and for charting new courses of action. Some of the most important approaches are outlined in the next few sections of this chapter.

Discovering Strengths and Weaknesses

One of your most important tasks in the following pages will be to get better acquainted with yourself. The best way to do so is to focus on your **strengths**. Through a series of useful self-assessment exercises and tests (Chapter 4, 6, and 7), you can identify your major strengths – those things you do well and enjoy doing. The theory behind this approach is very straightforward and appeals to common sense: You will most enjoy doing in the future what you have most enjoyed doing in the past. Discovering and following your most positive patterns will lead to wise career decisions and long-term job and career satisfaction. In its most extreme predictive form, this approach can lead to an uninspired conclusion – your future will most likely be a repeat of your past.

Failures and difficult times may have a greater impact on one's attitudes and motivations than successes.

Your present job may not be using your major strengths. In fact, you may discover that your major strengths are associated with your hobbies, sports activities, or volunteer work. Once you identify what you do well and enjoy doing, which also provides important clues to your motivations and patterns of achievements, you should be able to articulate what you will most enjoy doing in the future. Indeed, you should be in an excellent position to chart a new direction in your career and life.

This approach is always easier said than done and is not without its own set of difficulties. The problems are two-fold. First, strengths are normally defined as stories of success. You are supposed to learn a great deal about yourself from analyzing your successes. However, important lessons about oneself also can be learned from analyzing one's failures or how one coped with difficult situations. Indeed, failures and difficult times may have a greater impact on one's attitudes and motivations than successes. If, for example, you were fired from a job, you may interpret that experience as a failure. As most entrepreneurs will admit, the fear of failure can be a great motivator in determining certain types of behaviors, especially a constant drive to succeed. As a result, you may place greater value on job security and avoid taking risks that could get you into trouble on the job – even though an analysis of your strengths indicates that taking initiative and being creative are your major strengths! How you cope with difficult times, such as a layoff, illness, death, divorce, bankruptcy, or incarceration can be life-changing. Such experiences often result in drawing on surprising inner strengths that have nothing to do with planning and analysis. Learning how you coped with adversity can be very instructive in clarifying what you want to do in the future.

Second, learning about one's strengths can lead to a very deterministic approach to the future. In fact, this strategy is widely practiced by a particular group of career counselors who believe in the power of pre-destination, the magic of testing, and the predictive power of probability. Many come from pastoral counseling backgrounds that continue to direct their thinking about career choices and behavior. This approach is clearly articulated by Richard Nelson Bolles (***What Color Is Your Parachute?***, ***Three Boxes of Life***, and ***How to Find Your Mission in Life***), Arthur Miller and Ralph Mattson (***The Truth About You***), Richard Leider (***The Power of Purpose***), and Rick Warren (***The Purpose-Driven Life***), and espoused by a legion of career counselors raised on the theories of these popular writers/practitioners/gurus. Basic to this approach is both a deterministic and probabilistic theory of individual behavior – your future performance will most likely be a repeat of your past patterns of behavior. Major proponents justify using this approach on explicit religious grounds: Since God has put his imprint on you, and you cannot escape your fate, you need to discover what he has preordained for you. This approach ostensibly uncovers God's vision for you in the form of a "map," "calling," "path," "mission," or "purpose." Much of their work is based on the pioneering work of Haldane and Crystal (see Germann and Arnold's ***Bernard Haldane Associates Job and Career Building***, and Barkley and Sandburg's ***The Crystal-Barkley Guide to Taking Charge of Your Career***). A recent popular version of this approach is represented in Marcus Buckingham's ***Now, Discover Your Strengths***. The works of Stephen R. Covey, especially ***The 7 Habits of Highly Effective People*** and ***The 8ᵗʰ Habit: From Excellence to Greatness***, reinforce these strategies.

> *This approach is practiced by those who believe in the power of predestination, the magic of testing, and the predictive power of probability.*

This deterministic/predestination approach takes you down a narrow and often pessimistic road where you are advised to be "realistic" about your future. An analysis of historical data on you – rather than information on your future aspirations – should determine where you will go in the future. By discovering your past patterns of motivated abilities and skills, you will be able to formulate realistic career goals as well as an appropriate job search action plan.

Despite claims of effectiveness, laced with some religious and spiritual concepts, most self-assessment devices using this deterministic approach are designed to reconstruct your past "patterns" of work behavior and then project them into the future in the form of objectives or goals. Not a bad strategy for 80 percent of the population, but it does have its limitations for many individuals who are attempting to transcend their pasts and change their lives.

Personality Types, Typologies, and Fitness

Related to the strength and pattern approach is a personality "type" theory based on the work of psychologist Carl Gustav Jung and developed into testing applications by the mother/daughter team of Katherine Briggs and Isabel Briggs Myers (*Myers-Briggs Type Indicator®*). Their personality-type test is among those most commonly used by career counselors and experts. It's well represented in the works of Paul D. Tieger and Barbara Barron-Tieger (*Do What You Are*), Nicholas Lore (*The Pathfinder*), Donna Dunning (*What's Your Type of Career?*), Renee Baron (*What Type Am I?*), and Jean Kummerow, Linda Kirby, and Nancy Barger (*WORKTypes*). It's a fascinating strategy because of the strong appeal of personality theories of behavior, which most people can easily relate to. It also uses simplistic typologies for classifying individuals into different psychological types. For example, responding to a series of questions, individuals discover their personality type or code, such as an ESFP ("Responder"), which tells them how they best handle information, make decisions, and communicate with others.

Similar to the determinism underlying other approaches, this personality type approach views personality as a blueprint. In its simplest form, this method assures individuals that if they know and recognize their personality type, they should be better able to find their perfect job or career, one that is receptive to their particular personality type. They need to understand which types of personalities best "fit" into particular jobs that are most suited to such personalities. Focusing on personality "fitness," this is still a deterministic approach – you can't escape your past personality patterns that ostensibly translate into future on-the-job personality and behavioral patterns.

Other career writers develop similar typologies and classification systems using psychological indicators and interest and value inventories for describing, explaining, predicting, and prescribing career choices. Creating intellectually interesting classification systems for better understanding how individuals choose careers and behave in the workplace (description and explanation), they often confuse their analytical constructs with reality and then make a critical and unwarranted leap into predicting and prescribing career choices for individuals. Such classification systems take on a life and reality of their own when they move from description and explanation to prediction and prescription. An example of such an intellectual exercise involving a unique classification system that goes on to prescribe career choices is Martin Yate's "professional competencies" and "personal preferences" methodology (*Beat the Odds* and *CareerSmarts: Jobs With a Future*). At best an interesting exercise, it, too, uses a deterministic/predestination approach.

> *These approaches take you down that same sobering path – you are what you are; you'll be what you have already been regardless of your dreams and goals.*

Whether working with interests, skills, abilities, values, or personality as predictors of career choices, career satisfaction, or even job performance, each of these deterministic/predestination approaches basically takes you down that same sobering path which actually becomes a hall of mirrors – you are what you are; you'll be what you have already been regardless of your dreams and goals.

Attitudes, Dreams, and Self-Transformation

Another interesting approach focuses on attitudes, dreams, passions, self-transformation, and self-motivation. While this strategy is not used by many career counselors, its elements are often apparent in discussions of goal setting, networking, and handling rejections. You'll find numerous books, audiotapes, videos, and software specializing in improving self esteem and developing positive thinking, especially for individuals in sales occupations, such as real estate, insurance, retail and direct sales. This approach is designed to transform people's thinking and perceptions by changing negative attitudes into enthusiastic, can-do, positive attitudes. The approach primarily focuses on the future rather than on the past. It is goal-oriented rather than pattern-oriented. It's a powerful approach that challenges the mind set of career counselors raised on testing traditions. According to this approach, success is largely a function of dogged pursuit of a vision against the odds.

One of the major themes underlying this strategy and attendant self-help products is that **you can change your life through attitude adjustment and positive thinking**. Individuals whose lives are troubled, for example, can literally transform themselves by changing their thinking in new and positive directions. This approach and its associated products are especially popular with sales personnel who must constantly stay motivated and positive in the face of making cold calls to strangers that result in numerous rejections – an analogous situation many job seekers find themselves in when marketing themselves to employers, who are basically strangers. Positive thinking keeps them motivated and helps them get through the day, the week, and the month, despite numerous rejections that would normally dissuade most people from continuing to pursue more sales calls that result in even more rejections.

One of the most important books on self-transformation through positive thinking is Napoleon Hill's **_Think and Grow Rich_**. This single book has had a tremendous influence on the development of the positive-thinking industry, which now includes hundreds of motivational speakers and gurus who produce numerous seminars, books, videos, DVDs, and audiotapes for the true believers. It includes such popular books and authors as these:

Napoleon Hill	■ _Success Through a Positive Mental Attitude_
Dr. Norman Vincent Peale	■ _The Power of Positive Thinking_ ■ _Six Attitudes for Winners_

Anthony Robbins	■ *Awaken the Giant Within* ■ *Live With Passion!* ■ *Personal Power* ■ *Unlimited Power*
Dr. Robert H. Schuller	■ *Be Happy Attitudes* ■ *You Can Become the Person You Want to Be*
Dale Carnegie	■ *How to Win Friends and Influence People*
Brian Tracy	■ *Create Your Own Future* ■ *Eat That Frog!* ■ *Focal Point* ■ *Maximum Achievement*
David Schwartz	■ *The Magic of Thinking Big*
Zig Ziglar	■ *How to Get What You Want*
Og Mandino	■ *Secrets of Success*
Steve Chandler	■ *100 Ways to Motivate Yourself* ■ *Reinventing Yourself*
Bay and Macpherson	■ *Change Your Attitude*
Keith Harrell	■ *Attitude Is Everything*

Three recent books also focus on pursuing one's dreams and passions rather than analyzing one's past: Po Bronson, **What Should I Do With My Life?**; Sharon Cook and Graciela Sholander, **Dream It Do It**; and Paul and Sarah Edwards, **Practical Dreamer's Handbook**. Any of these books will get you started on the road to changing your attitudes as well as your life. They are filled with fascinating stories of self-transformation, motivational language, and exercises for developing positive attitudes for success.

You'll be much wiser in your job search, and on your job, if you read and re-read a few of these motivational books.

While this positive thinking and motivational approach appeals to many people, especially those in sales and other risk-taking professionals, its effectiveness is by no means certain. Individuals often achieve a temporary attitude enhancement high, but they later have difficulty making significant changes in their behavior patterns.

Rejections and Motivation

As you will quickly discover, rejections and motivation go hand in hand. After all, the whole process of identifying what you want to do and charting a course of action consists of very ego-involved activities where your whole sense of self-worth is on the line. If, for example, you are especially sensitive to rejections, you may have difficulty maintaining a positive attitude, expressing enthusiasm, and remaining motivated and focused. Indeed, some job seekers become very depressed while looking for a job.

How you handle rejections may largely determine how successful you will be in your job search.

How you handle rejections may largely determine how successful you will be in charting new courses of action that involve communicating with strangers. Most individuals are not prepared to deal with the many rejections attendant with conducting a job search. After the fourth rejection, for example, many people become disillusioned in finding a job. Some give up and lament their situation by saying *"No one will hire me!"* However, a typical job search goes something like this:

> No, No, No, No, No, No, No, No, No, No, Maybe, No, No, No
> No, No, No, Maybe, No, No, No, No, Maybe, No, No, No, Yes

If you get disillusioned and quit after receiving four rejections, you will prematurely fail. You need to continue "collecting" more rejections in order to get to acceptances. In fact, we often recommend that individuals get up in the morning with the idea of collecting at least 20 rejections! You will eventually get acceptances, but you must first deal with many rejections on the road to success.

How you deal with rejections may largely determine how successful you will be in pursuing something else in your career and life. If you identify what it is you want to do but cannot implement the necessary changes because you fear rejection, you will be going nowhere with your future.

3

Working With Your
Best Friends

W E ALL NEED FRIENDS when it comes time to look for a job or change careers. Friends represent familiarity and camaraderie, provide important psychological supports, and often give useful information, advice, and referrals. Your friend can be a buddy, a girl/boy friend, spouse, relative, a former school mate, or teacher who shares important information and advice as well as contacts that can lead to a job interview and offer. Your friend also can be a seasoned career professional who provides important structure, motivation, and support for implementing your job search and landing your dream job. Whatever the case, you should consider acquiring and using as many friends as possible in clarifying what you want to do with whom in the future.

Communicating With Friends

Don't be afraid to talk to friends and associates about your interests, goals, and career plans, even if you have lost your job. Cast as broad an information net as you can. Most of your friends and associates will be interested in what you are doing. Some may even confide in you the fact that they, too, would like to be doing what you are doing – exploring new job and career options. In fact, you may end up creating a support group of individuals who want to join together in discovering what else they would like to do with their lives!

Unfortunately, many individuals try to keep their job and career interests a secret from the very people who might be most helpful. Consider sharing a statement similar to the following with your friends:

> *I've decided I would like to do something else with my life. Over the next few months I'm going to explore some new job and career options. If you don't mind, I may want to ask you for some advice.*

This statement should elicit some interesting responses. You'll discover that many of your friends can relate to your career situation. At some point they probably encountered a similar situation about their career and life. Not surprisingly, most of your friends will be happy to give you free advice. Some will provide excellent referrals to other individuals who will offer you useful information, advice, and referrals. This whole process is what we mean by **networking** – building, maintaining, and extending connections to others for the purposes of acquiring useful information, advice, and referrals and for being remembered for future reference.

> *Friends represent familiarity and camaraderie, provide important psychological supports, and often give useful information, advice, and referrals.*

As you share your story with friends and associates, you will be building an important **support network** for achieving your goals. Best of all, you'll be **minimizing rejections** by talking to the very people who are willing to help you shape your future. As you gather information, advice, and referrals, you'll learn a great deal about yourself, others, the job market, jobs, careers, and employers. You'll get a better sense of what you want to do, because you have a better understanding of job and career realities that relate to your goals, interests, skills, and abilities.

Be careful in how you present your story to friends and associates. At no time should you try to use friends to get ahead. Share your story and ask for advice. Never ask a friend or associate to find you employment.

Once you do that, you cross a fine line that could damage your relationships. While most people are happy to give you advice, few people want to be put upon to take responsibility for your employment fate. Those that do will most likely charge you money, which we'll discuss shortly.

On Your Own and With Others

You have two options in planning your future and organizing an effective job search. First, you can follow the principles and advice outlined in this and many other self-directed books. Just read the chapters and then put them into practice by following the step-by-step instructions. The assumption here is that you are a highly motivated self-starter who just needs some how-to advice and direction to do everything on your own. Not a bad assumption, but it's probably only valid for 10 percent of the population who can successfully do everything on their own, from planning to implementation. The planning or pre-implementation process is probably the easiest for you to do on your own. You can assess your skills, develop an objective, conduct research, and write resumes and letters on your own.

> *Most people have difficulty implementing a career plan, because they lack a structure for implementation – a career coach, advisor, or support group.*

But when it comes time to implement your plan of action, which involves networking and contacting many potential employers, you may encounter numerous difficulties doing it on your own. In addition to the problem of rejections, which we noted at the end of Chapter 2, most people have difficulty implementing a career plan, because they lack a structure for implementation. That structure often comes in the form of a career coach, advisor, or support group that can help individuals through the ego-bruising ups and downs of the career planning and job search processes. Without such a structure, you may end up becoming disillusioned as you wander aimlessly in a sea of rejections. Failing to do first things first, you may make many implementation errors commonly associated with ineffective job searches, such as writing your resume first, spending an inordinate amount of time looking for jobs on the Internet, or responding to classified ads, and failing to network and properly follow up. Just because you understand a process does not mean you also are capable of implementing that process.

Second, you may wish to seek professional help to either supplement or replace this book. Indeed, many people will read parts of this book – perhaps all of it – and do nothing. They may read several other how-to books and again do nothing. Some will even spend money attending motivational, career planning, and job search seminars and again do nothing. Lacking sufficient time or motivation beyond the moment it takes to read the book or attend the seminar, or failing to follow through, many people eventually seek professional help to organize and implement their job search. Hopefully, they will work with a career professional or career coach who can provide them with assistance in completing each step outlined in this book. Such assistance results in creating a structure for implementation.

We recognize the value of professional assistance. Especially with the critical assessment and objective-setting steps (Chapters 6, 7, and 8), some individuals may need more assistance than our advice and exercises provide. You may, for example, want to take a battery of tests to better understand your interests and values in relation to alternative jobs and careers. And still others, due to a combination of job loss, failed relationships, or depression, may need therapy best provided by a trained psychologist or psychiatrist rather than career testing and information services provided by career counselors. If any of these situations pertain to you, by all means seek professional help.

Beware of Pitfalls in Hiring a Professional

You also should beware of pitfalls in seeking professional advice. While many services are excellent, some services are useless and fraudulent. Remember, career planning and job assistance are big businesses involving millions of dollars each year. Many people enter these businesses without expertise. Professional certification in these areas is extremely weak to non-existent in some states. Indeed, many so-called "professionals" get into the business because they are unemployed. In other words, they major in their own problem! Others are frauds and hucksters who prey on vulnerable and naive people who feel they need a "specialist" or "expert" to get them a job. They will take your money in exchange for promises.

You will find several types of services promising to assist you in finding all types of jobs. You should know something about these professional services before you venture beyond this book.

If you are interested in exploring the services of job specialists, begin by looking in the Yellow Pages of your telephone directory under these headings: Management Consultants, Employment, Resumes, Career Planning, and Social Services. You also should check out a few websites of certified career professionals, which we recommend near the end of this chapter. Several career planning and employment services are available, ranging from highly generalized to very specific services. Most services claim they can help you. If you read this book, you will be in a better position to seek out specific services as well as ask the right questions for screening the services. You may even discover you know more about finding a job than many of the so-called professionals!

> *Beware: While many career services are excellent, some services are useless and fraudulent.*

Seeking Professional Assistance

At least 12 different types of career planning and employment services are available to assist you with different phases of your job search. Most of these services include some type of career assessment activity, from self-directed exercises to pencil-and-paper tests. Many rely heavily on the two most popular assessment devices – *Myers-Briggs Type Indicator*® and *Strong Interest Inventory*®.

Each of these services has certain advantages and disadvantages. Approach them with caution. Always remember that career planning is a big and largely unregulated business where you will occasionally encounter hucksters and fraudulent services aimed at taking advantage of individuals who are psychologically vulnerable and naive. Many of these hucksters self-certify themselves, promise to locate jobs that pay more than your last one, and seal the deal by asking for up-front money – $500 to $15,000 – to find you a job. Lacking good shopping sense and engaging in wishful thinking, many job seekers fall for the false promises of these so-called employment experts.

Our advice is very simple: Never sign a contract before you read the fine print, get a second opinion, and talk to former clients about the **results** they achieved through the service. While most of these services are not free, there is no reason to believe that the most expensive services are the best services. In fact, you may get the same quality of services from a group that charges $300 versus one that costs $15,000. At the same time, free or cheap services are not necessarily as good as the more expensive services. While you often get what you pay for in this industry, you also may get much less than what you pay for. Again, before using any employment services or hiring an expert, do your research by contacting a few individuals who have used the services.

With these words of caution in mind, let's examine a variety of services available, which you may or may not want to incorporate in your career planning and job search efforts.

1. **Public employment services**

Public employment services usually consist of a state agency which provides employment assistance as well as dispenses unemployment compensation benefits. Employment assistance largely consists of job listings and counseling services. However, counseling services often screen individuals for employers who list with the public employment agency. If you are looking for an entry-level job or a job paying $18,000 to $40,000, contact these services. Most employers still do not list with them, especially for positions paying more than $40,000 a year. Although the main purpose of these offices has been to dispense unemployment benefits, don't overlook them because of past stereotypes. The Workforce Development Act has re-energized such services. Within the past four years, many of these offices have literally "reinvented" themselves for today's new job market with One-Stop Career Centers, computerized job banks, counseling services, training programs, and other innovative organizational and technical approaches. Many of them offer useful employment services, including self-assessment and job search workshops as well as access to job listings on the Internet. Most of these offices are linked to America's Job Bank (www.ajb.dni.us), an electronic job bank which includes over 1 million job listings throughout the U.S. and abroad. This is one of the premier employment websites that offers a wealth of information and resources for job seekers. It's one all job seekers need to become familiar with. America's Job Bank, in turn, is linked to the U.S. Department of Labor's three other useful websites – America's CareerInfoNet (www.acinet.org), America's Service Locator (www.servicelocator.org), and Career OneStop (www.careeronestop.org). If you are a veteran, you will find many of the jobs listed with state employment offices give veterans preference in hiring. Go see for yourself if your state employment office offers useful services for you.

2. Private employment agencies

Private employment agencies work for money, either from applicants or employers. Approximately 8,000 such agencies operate nation-wide. Many are highly specialized in technical, scientific, and financial fields. The majority of these firms serve the interests of employers, since employers – not applicants – represent repeat business. While employers normally pay the placement fee, many agencies charge applicants 10 to 15 percent of their first year salary. These firms have one major advantage: job leads which you may have difficulty uncovering elsewhere. Especially for highly special-ized fields, a good firm can be extremely helpful. The major disad-vantages are that they can be costly and the quality of the firms varies. Be careful in how you deal with them. Make sure you under-stand the fee structure and what they will do for you before you sign anything. The bi-annual directory *JobBank Guide to Employment Services* (Adams Media) includes data on nearly 3,000 firms.

3. Temporary staffing firms

During the past decade temporary staffing firms have come of age as more and more employers turn to them for recruitment assistance. They offer a variety of employment services to both applicants and employers who are either looking for temporary work and workers or who want to better screen applicants and employers. Many of these firms, such as Manpower (www.manpower.com), Olsten (www.olsten.com), and Kelly Services (www.kellyservices.com), recruit individuals for a wide range of positions and skill levels as well as full-time employment. Some firms, such as Robert Half International (www.rhii.com) specialize in certain types of workers (accounting, law, information technology, or computer personnel). If you are interested in "testing the job waters," you may want to contact these firms for information on their services. Employers – not job seekers – pay for these services. While many of these firms are listed in the Yellow Pages, most have websites. The following websites are especially popular with individuals interested in part-time or contract work: www.net-temps.com, www.elance.com, www.ework. com, www.guru.com, www.contractorforum.com, and www.talent market.monster.com,

4. College/university placement offices

College and university placement offices provide in-house career planning services for graduating students. While some give assistance to alumni, don't expect too much help if you have already graduated; you may, instead, need to contact the alumni office which may offer employment services. Many college placement offices are understaffed or provide only rudimentary services, such as maintaining a career planning library, coordinating on-campus interviews for graduating seniors, and conducting workshops on how to write resumes and interview. Others provide a full range of well supported services including testing and one-on-one counseling. Indeed, many community colleges offer such services to members of the community on a walk-in basis. You can use their libraries and computerized career assessment programs, take personality and interest inventories, or attend special workshops or full-semester career planning courses which will take you through each step of the career planning and job search processes. You may want to enroll in such a course since it is likely to provide just enough structure and content to assess your motivated abilities and skills and to assist you in implementing a successful job search plan. Check with your local campus to see what services you might use. Many of the college and university placement offices belong to the National Association of Colleges and Employers, which operates its own employment website: www.jobweb.com. This site includes a wealth of information on employment for college graduates (see the "Site Map" section: www.jobweb.com/search/sitemap.htm). Its "Career Library" section includes direct links to hundreds of college and university placement offices: www.jobweb.com/Career-Development/collegeres.htm. To find college alumni offices, visit the following websites: www.alumni. net, www.bcharrispub.com, and www.jobweb.com/After_College. Since colleges and universities tend to be very web-savvy, you can visit hundreds of their career websites to acquire all types of useful free information on conducting an effective job search. One of our favorites is the website operated by the Career Center at the College of William and Mary (www.wm.edu/career). Indeed, searching many of these college and university websites is comparable to having your own personal career counselor – without having to go to college!

5. Private career and job search firms

Private career and job search firms help individuals acquire job search skills and coach them through the process of finding a job. They do not find you a job. In other words, they teach you much of what is outlined in this book. Expect to pay anywhere from $1,500 to $10,000 for this service. If you need a structured environment for conducting your job search, contract with one of these firms for professional assistance. One of the major such firms used to be Bernard Haldane Associates (they ceased operating under that name and became BH Careers International, www.bhcareers.com, in 2004). Many of their pioneering career planning and job search methods are incorporated in this book as well as can be found in five other key job search books: *Haldane's Best Resumes for Professionals*, *Haldane's Best Cover Letters for Professionals*, *Haldane's Best Answers to Tough Interview Questions*, *Haldane's Best Salary Tips for Professionals*, and *Haldane's Best Employment Websites for Professionals* (Impact Publications – see the order form at the end of this book or www.impactpublications.com). Other firms offering similar services include Right Management Consultants (www.right. com), R. L. Stevens & Associates (www.interviewing.com), and Lee Hecht Harrison (www.lhh.com/us).

6. Executive search firms and headhunters

Executive search firms work for employers in finding employees to fill critical positions in the $50,000 plus salary range. They also are called "headhunters," "management consultants," and "executive recruiters." These firms play an important role in linking high level technical and managerial talent to organizations. Don't expect to contract for these services. Executive recruiters work for employers, not applicants. If a friend or relative is in this business or you have relevant skills of interest to these firms, let them know you are available – and ask for their advice. On the other hand, you may want to contact firms that specialize in recruiting individuals with your skill specialty. For a comprehensive listing of these firms, see the latest annual edition of *The Directory of Executive Recruiters* (Kennedy Information, www.kennedyinfo.com; also see the order form at the end of this book and www.impactpublications.com). Several companies, such as www.resumezapper.com, www.blastmyresume.com, and www.resumeblaster.com, offer e-mail resume blasting services that primarily target headhunters. For a fee, which usually ranges from $50 to $200, these firms will blast your resume to 5,000 to 10,000 headhunters. This is a quick, easy, and inexpensive way to reach thousands of headhunters and executive search firms. This resume distribution method also may be a waste of time and money. Approach it with a sense of healthy skepticism.

7. Marketing services

Marketing services represent an interesting combination of job search and executive search activities. They can cost $2,500 or more, and they work with individuals anticipating a starting salary of at least $75,000 but preferably over $100,000. These firms try to minimize the time and risk of applying for jobs. A typical operation begins with a client paying a $150 fee for developing psychological, skills, and interests profiles. If you pass this stage – most anyone with money does – you go on to the next one-on-one stage. At this point, a marketing plan is outlined and a contract signed for specific services. Work for the clients usually involves activities centered on the resume and interviewing. Using word processing software, the firm normally develops a slick "professional" resume and sends it by mail or e-mail, along with a cover letter, to hundreds – maybe thousands – of firms. Clients are then briefed and sent to interview with interested employers. While you can save money and achieve the same results on your own, these firms do have one major advantage: They save you **time** by doing most of the work for you. Again, approach these services with caution and with the knowledge that you can probably do just as well – if not better – on your own by following the step-by-step advice of this and other job search books.

8. Women's centers and special career services

Women's centers and special career services for displaced workers, such as 40-Plus Clubs (www.40plus.org/chapters) and Five O'Clock Clubs (www.fiveoclockclub.com), have been established to respond to the employment needs of special groups. Women's centers are particularly active in sponsoring career planning workshops and job information networks. These centers tend to be geared toward elementary job search activities, because many of their clientele consist of homemakers who are entering or re-entering the work force with little knowledge of the job market. Special career services arise at times for different categories of employees. For example, unemployed aerospace engineers, teachers, veterans, air traffic controllers, and government employees have formed special groups for developing job search skills and sharing job leads.

9. Testing and assessment centers

Testing and assessment centers provide assistance for identifying vocational skills, interests, and objectives. Usually staffed by trained professionals, these centers administer several types of tests and charge from $200 to $900 per person. We summarize most of these tests and inventories in Chapter 4. You may wish to use some of these services if you feel our activities in Chapters 6-8 generate insufficient information on your skills and interests to formulate your job objective. If you use such services, make sure you are given one or both of the two most popular and reliable tests: *Myers-Briggs Type Indicator*® and the *Strong Interest Inventory*®. You should find both tests helpful in better understanding your interests and decision-making styles. However, try our exercises in the following chapters before you hire a psychologist or visit a testing center. If you first complete these exercises, you will be in a better position to know exactly what you need from such centers. In many cases, the career office at your local community college or women's center can administer these tests at minimum cost ($20 to $40). At the same time, many of these testing and assessment services are now available online. Check out these popular websites: www.skillsone. com, www.self-directed-search.com, www.careerlab.com, www.per sonalityonline.com, www.assessment.com, and www.personalitytype. com.

10. Job fairs and career conferences

Job fairs and career conferences are organized by a variety of groups – from schools and government agencies to headhunters, employment agencies, and professional associations – to link applicants to employers. **Job fairs** are often open to the public and involve many employers. **Career conferences** may be closed to the public (invitation only) and involve a single employer. Usually consisting of one- to two-day meetings in a hotel or conference center, employers meet with applicants as a group and on a one-to-one basis. Employers give presentations on their companies, applicants circulate resumes, and employers interview candidates. Many such conferences are organized to attract hard-to-recruit groups, such as engineers, computer programmers, individuals with security clearances, and clerical and service workers, or for special population groups, such as minorities, transitioning military personnel, women, people with disabilities, and even ex-offenders. These are excellent sources for job leads and information on specific employers and jobs – if you are invited to attend or if the meeting is open to the public. Employers pay for this service, although some job fairs and career conferences may charge job seekers a nominal registration fee.

11. Professional associations

Professional associations often provide placement assistance. This usually consists of listing job vacancies in publications, maintaining a resume database, and organizing a job information exchange at annual conferences. Some may even organize job fairs, such as the Military Officers Association (www.moaa.org) and the Non-Commissioned Officers Association (www.ncoausa.org). Many large associations operate their own online employment sites; members can include their resume in an electronic database and employers can access the database to search for qualified candidates. Annual conferences are good sources for making job contacts in different geographic locations within a particular professional field. But don't expect too much. Talking to people (networking) at professional conferences may yield better results than reading job listings, placing your resume online, or interviewing at conference placement centers. For excellent online directories of professional associations, be sure to visit these two sites: www.ipl.org/ref/AON and www.asaenet.org.

12. Professional resume writers

Professional resume writers are increasingly playing an important role in career planning. Each year thousands of job seekers rely on these professionals for assistance in writing their resumes. Many of these professionals also provide useful job search tips on resume distribution, cover letters, and networking as well as include other career planning and job search services, such as assessment, mentoring, and practice interviewing. Charging from $100 to $600 for writing a resume, they work with the whole spectrum of job seekers – entry-level to senior executives making millions of dollars each year. While some are certified career counselors, many of these professionals have their own associations and certification groups that include a large assortment of often unintelligible initials after their names – CAC, CBC, CCM, CEIP, CHRE, CIPC, CPC, CPRW, JCTC, LPC, NBCC, NCC, NCCC, NCRW, and PCC. If you are interested in working with a professional resume writer, visit the following websites for information on this network of career professionals: www.parw.com, www.prwra.com, www.cminstitute.com, and www.nrwaweb.com. Examples of their high-end work can be found in Wendy Enelow's two books: *Best Resumes for $100,000+ Jobs* and *Best Cover Letters for $100,000+ Jobs* (Impact Publications – see order form at the end of this book or visit the publisher's online bookstore: www.impactpublications.com).

Finding Certified Career Professionals

Certified career professionals are experienced in working one-on-one with clients, with special emphasis on career assessment. They have their own professional associations. If you are interested in contacting a certified career professional for assistance, we advise you to first visit these websites for locating a career professional:

- **National Board for Certified Counselors, Inc.**   www.nbcc.org
- **National Career Development Association**   www.ncda.org
- **Certified Career Coaches**   www.certifiedcareer coaches.com
- **Career Planning and Adult Development Network**   www.careernetwork.org

You also can find a great deal of professional career assistance through the U.S. Department of Labor's website, which enables users to locate services within their communities:

- **America's Service Locator**   www.servicelocator.org

Working With the Best

Other types of career planning and employment services are growing and specializing in particular occupational fields. You may wish to use these services as a supplement to this book.

Whatever you do, be a smart shopper for career planning and job search services. Proceed with caution, know exactly what you are getting into, and choose the best. Remember, there is no such thing as a free lunch, and you often get less than what you pay for. At the same time, the most expensive services are not necessarily the best. Indeed, the free and inexpensive career planning services offered by many community or junior colleges – libraries, computerized career assessment programs, testing, and workshops – may be all you need. On the other hand, don't be afraid to spend some money on getting the best services. You may quickly discover that this money was well spent when you land a job that pays 20 to 40 percent more than your previous job! Whatever you do, don't be *"pennywise but pound foolish"* by trying to do your job search on the cheap. If you have difficulty writing a first-class resume, by all means contact a resume-writing pro who can put together a dynamite resume that truly represents what you have done, can do, and will do in the future.

After reading this book, you should be able to make intelligent decisions about what, when, where, and with what results you can use professional assistance. Shop around, compare services and costs, ask questions, talk to former clients, and read the fine print before giving an employment expert a job using your hard earned money. Don't try to be the Lone Ranger all of the time. If necessary, contact a career professional at different stages of your job search. A career expert could very well become your best friend in the process of deciding exactly what you want to do in the future!

> *Don't try to be the Lone Ranger all of the time. If necessary, contact a career professional at different stages of your job search.*

Useful Job Clubs and Support Groups

The techniques outlined thus far are designed for individuals conducting a self-directed job search. Job clubs and support groups are two important alternatives to these techniques.

Job clubs are designed to provide a group structure and support system to individuals seeking employment. These groups consist of about 12 individuals who are led by a trained counselor and supported with telephones, copying machines, and a resource center.

Formal job clubs, such as the 40-Plus Clubs (www.40plus.org/chapters) and the Five O'Clock Clubs (www.fiveoclockclub.com), organize job search activities for both the advertised and hidden job markets. Job club activities may include:

- Signing commitment agreements to achieve specific job search goals and targets.

- Contacting friends, relatives, and acquaintances for job leads.

- Completing activity forms.

- Using telephones, computers, photocopy machines, postage, and other equipment and supplies.

- Meeting with fellow participants to discuss job search progress.

- Meeting with career counselors or other career specialists.

- Attending job fairs and hiring conferences.

- Telephoning to uncover job leads.

- Using the Internet to research the job market and contact potential employers.

- Researching newspapers, telephone books, and directories.

- Developing research, telephone, interview, and social skills.

- Writing letters and resumes.

- Responding to want ads.

- Completing employment applications.

- Assessing weekly progress and sharing information with fellow group members.

In other words, the job club formalizes many of the prospecting, networking, and informational interviewing activities within a group context and interjects the role of the telephone as the key communication device for developing and expanding networks.

Many job clubs place excessive reliance on using the telephone and Internet for uncovering job leads. Members call prospective employers and ask about job openings. The Yellow Pages and the Internet become the job hunter's best friends. During a two-week period, a job club member might spend most mornings telephoning for job leads and scheduling interviews. Afternoons are normally devoted to interviewing.

Many job club methods are designed for individuals who need a job – any job – quickly. Since individuals try to fit into available vacancies, their specific objectives and skills are of secondary concern. Other job club methods are more consistent with the focus and methods outlined in this book, especially those used by 40-Plus Clubs and Five O'Clock Clubs.

In lieu of participating in such clubs, you may want to form your own **support group** that adapts some job club methods around our central concept of finding a job fit for you – one appropriate to your objective and in line with your particular mix of skills, abilities, and interests. Support groups are a useful alternative to job clubs. They have one major advantage to conducting a job search on your own: they may cut your job search time in half because they provide an important structure for achieving goals. Forming or joining one of these groups can help direct as well as enhance your individual job search activities.

> *Job search clubs may cut your job search time in half because they provide an important structure for achieving goals.*

Your support group should consist of three or more individuals who are job hunting. Try to schedule regular meetings with specific purposes in mind. While the group may be highly social, especially if it involves close friends, it also should be **task-oriented**. Meet at least once a week and include your spouse. At each meeting set **performance goals** for the week. For example, your goal can be to make 20 new contacts and conduct five informational interviews. The contacts can be made by telephone, e-mail, letter, or in person. Share your experiences and job information with each other. **Critique** each other's progress, make suggestions for improving the job search, and develop new strategies together. By doing this, you will be gaining valuable information and feedback which is normally difficult to gain on one's own. This group should provide important psychological supports to help you through your job search. After all, job hunting can be a lonely, frustrating, and exasperating experience. By sharing your experiences with others, you will find you are not alone. You will quickly learn that rejections are part of the game. The group will encourage you, and you will feel good about helping others achieve their goals. Try building small incentives into the group, such as the individual who receives the most job interviews for the month will be treated to dinner by other members of the group.

Online Networking Resources

Networking is increasingly taking on new communication forms in today's high-tech world. Job seekers can take advantage of several websites and electronic databases for conducting a job search, from gathering information on the job market to disseminating resumes to employers. The Internet also allows job seekers to network for information, advice, and job leads. If you belong to one of the major Internet service providers, such as America Online, or have direct access to the Internet's World Wide Web, you can use mailing lists, news groups, bulletin boards, blogs, chat groups, message boards, and e-mail to gather job information and make contacts with potential employers. Using e-mail, you can make personal contacts which give you job leads for further networking via computer or through the more traditional networking methods outlined in this chapter.

Several websites will help you develop networking skills as well as put you in contact with important employment-related networks. These sites include a wealth of information on the networking process:

- **WetFeet**   www.wetfeet.com/advice/
                                    networking.asp
- **Monster.com**   http://networking.monster.com
- **Quintessential Careers**   www.quintcareers.com/
                                    networking.html
- **Riley Guide**   www.rileyguide.com/netintv.html
- **WinningTheJob**   www.winningthejob.com
- **SchmoozeMonger**   www.schmoozemonger.com
- **Susan RoAne**   www.susanroane.com/free.html
- **Contacts Count**   www.contactscount.com/articles.
                                    html

One you begin the process of developing your networks, you may want to use the following websites to locate long-lost friends, classmates, and others who might be helpful in your networking campaign:

- **Anywho**   www.anywho.com
- **Classmates**   www.classmates.com
- **InfoSpace**   www.infospace.com

- KnowX   www.knowx.com
- Reunion (high school)   www.reunion.com
- Switchboard   www.switchboard.com
- The Ultimate White Pages   www.theultimates.com/white
- People Search Lycos   www.whowhere.lycos.com
- Yahoo   www.people.yahoo.com

If you have military experience and wish to locate some of your former military buddies, be sure to explore these people finders for locating military personnel:

- GI Search.com   www.gisearch.com
- Military.com   www.military.com
- Military Connections   www.militaryconnections.com
- MilitaryUSA.com   www.militaryusa.com

If you've lost contact with your former classmates, try these websites for locating alumni groups:

- Alumni.net   www.alumni.net
- Curious Cat Alumni
  Connections   www.curiouscat.net/alumni

Many women's groups organize networking opportunities among their members for career development purposes. The following organizations are especially relevant to female networkers:

- Advancing Women   www.advancingwomen.com
- American Association of
  University Women   www.aauw.org
- American Business
  Women's Association   www.abwahq.org
- Systers   www.www.systers.org
- Business Women's
  Network   www.bwni.com
- Federally Employed Women   www.few.org
- iVillage   www.ivillage.com

- Women.com   www.women.com
- Womans.net   www.womans-net.com

Business professionals will find these three networking groups of special interest because they sponsor special online and off line networking events:

- Company of Friends   http://fastcompany.com/cof
- ExecuNet   www.execunet.com
- Technology Executives
  Networking Group   www.theteng.org

Many of the large Internet employment sites maintain message boards. Two of the largest message board operations, which offer opportunities to network for information and advice, are found at these websites:

- Monster.com   http://networking.monster.com/
                                  board
- Vault.com   www.vault.com/community/mb/
                                  mb_home.jsp

The latest trend or fad in online networking is based upon the "six degrees of separation theory" – everyone is connected to everyone else in the world by only six other people. A somewhat dubious theory, nonetheless, these networks have been responsible for a great deal of news media hype since 2003 on how to expand one's network of connections for personal and professional purposes. Building electronic communities, these networks are designed to put users into contact with thousands of other people for all types of purposes – from dating to making friends to finding a job to recruiting to developing sales forces to closing business deals. The ultimate soft approach to cold calling, these electronic networks tend to be of questionable value to job seekers who have actually used them. After all, they formalize what is essentially an informal, personal process that works best in one degree removed face-to-face situations. Nonetheless, these new electronic networks offer some interesting online networking opportunities for those who have the time and dedication to make them work. They probably are most effective for those who need to prospect for new business and potential sales contacts, which is the direction many of the more entrepreneurial such networks now take. The following websites are devoted to promoting this type of networking activity:

- **LinkedIn**   www.linkedin.com
- **Friendster**   www.friendster.com
- **Ryze**   www.ryze.com
- **Spoke**   www.spoke.com
- **EntreMate**   www.entremate.com

The first website, www.linkedin.com, tends to be used by more job seekers and recruiters than the other networking sites. If you want to try your luck with this type of online networking in your job search, or if you are a recruiter seeking new talent, we recommend starting with LinkedIn.

The Internet can significantly enhance your job search. It offers new networking possibilities for individuals who are literate in today's digital technology. If you have access to the Internet, we recommend getting your resume into various employment websites. Explore their bulletin boards, chat groups, message boards, resources, and job vacancies. Within just a few minutes of electronic networking, you may pick up important job information, advice, and leads that could turn into a real job. For more information on online networking, see the electronic networking sections of our two books on networking and the Internet: *The Savvy Networker* and *America's Top Internet Job Sites* (Impact Publications).

Disappointing "In the Moment" Networking

While networking is often viewed as the best way to find new friends who can help you with your job search, don't become too enthusiastic or rely too heavily on this approach. Although networking is important for gathering information, advice, and referrals, its importance is often exaggerated. Indeed, in today's fast-paced world of multiple and superficial encounters, networking often becomes an "in the moment" phenomenon. Individuals you encounter as possible networking contacts often only give you a great deal of attention during your initial encounter – in the moment you meet. It could be a five-, 10-, or 15-minute conversation. You depart with the impression that you have formed a friendship or at least a good contact. But try to follow up on this new-found contact.

What you thought might become an important contact can quickly fade away as the initial encounter becomes a one-shot "you have my attention right now but not necessarily in the future" meeting. Indeed, many networking contacts quickly dissipate after the initial encounter. You may follow up your encounter, but chances are he or she either doesn't remember you or is too busy to give you attention, especially when your follow-up requires some work on the part of the contact. Like many of today's friendships, network contacts can become very superficial encounters that lead nowhere. Consider these to be dead-end encounters – entertaining during the initial meeting but useless thereafter.

4

The Magical World of Tests and Inventories

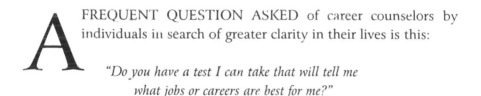

A FREQUENT QUESTION ASKED of career counselors by individuals in search of greater clarity in their lives is this:

*"Do you have a test I can take that will tell me
what jobs or careers are best for me?"*

This question is responsible for a huge, lucrative, and fascinating self-assessment industry that offers hundreds of paper-and-pencil, computerized, and Internet-based tests and inventories taken by millions of individuals, especially students at all levels, each year. Asked in this form, the answer to this question is both simple and complex: *"Yes, but . . ."* Sometimes this industry gives one the impression of peddling a scientific version of snake oil. You'll have to be your own judge based upon the actual results you get from taking such tests and inventories.

The Magic of Tests

There's something very appealing, almost magical, about taking computerized and/or pencil-and-paper psychological, career planning, and guidance tests and inventories that are designed to simplify reality. For some people, these tests are potentially the magic bullet to discovering what they should do with the rest of their life. By looking within themselves, rather that focusing outside (see our discussion in Chapter 2 about attitudes, dreams, and self-transformation), they believe they can find answers to important questions about their future. While no such bullet exists, nonetheless, these self-focused devices can be very useful at the initial stage of one's job search. Many who take these tests respond with a temporary *"Wow!"* or *"Aha!"* when they get the results and interpretations. Whether or not these tests have behavioral consequences (what you actually do with this information) is another question altogether.

> *These devices can be very useful at the initial stage of one's job search. Whether or not they have behavioral consequences for most users is another question altogether.*

Here's how most assessment tests and instruments work. You answer a series of questions about yourself (multiple-choice, true/false, Likert-type scale) and someone, usually a certified counselor, analyzes the results. If all goes well, an analysis will give you a general picture of who you really are in terms of your personality, interests, skills, abilities, aptitudes, and temperaments as well as evidence of where you may be going in the future, especially if the results are matched with specific jobs and careers. While many of these assessments have multiple applications – used for dealing with addictions, relationships, conflict, dating, parenting, educational choices, personnel growth, character, motivation, management styles, leadership, and organizational effectiveness – many of these same tests are used for career counseling, especially in reference to career choices.

Multiple Choices

You will encounter hundreds of career-related tests for assessing who you are, how you relate to others, and where you best fit into the future. Many of these tests are based on the psychological "type" theories and approaches of psychologist Carl Gustav Jung and popularized through the *Myers-Briggs Type Indicator®* and a variety of related applications. Other more vocational-oriented tests attempt to relate decision-making data to specific jobs and careers identified in the databases of the U.S. Department of Labor, especially the O*NET, as well as the job search process. Some of the most widely used assessment tests administered by career professionals include the following:

Personality and Motivation

- **California Psychological Inventory Form 434 (CPI™ 434):** Designed to assess personality characteristics behavioral tendencies across 3 Structural Scales, 20 Folk Scales, and 13 Special Purpose Scales. Used to determine psychological personality fit for employment and differences in management style, organizational impact, and team leadership. Available through Consulting Psychologists Press (www.cpp.com).

- **Edwards Personal Preference Schedule:** Assesses individual personality in reference to 15 needs and motives, such as achievement, order, affiliation, dominance, nurturance, endurance, and aggression. Available through The Psychological Corporation (http://harcourtassessment.com/hai/International.aspx).

- **Enneagram:** Analyzes nine distinct personality types in order to better understand individual personalities and how people relate to one another – Reformer, Helper, Achiever, Individualist, Investigator, Loyalist, Enthusiast, Challenger, and Peacemaker. Available through the Enneagram Institute(www.ennea graminstitute.com) and other sources such as www.ennea.com.

- **Keirsey Character Sorter:** This personality type approach is designed to analyze and apply the four basic "people pattern" temperaments, as developed in David Keirsey's popular book, *Please Understand Me II*, to different situations: Artisans, Guardians, Idealists, and Rationals. Available through David Mark Keirsey (http://keirsey.com).

- **Myers-Briggs Type Indicator® (MBTI®):** This is the most popular personality inventory in the world used by psychologists and career counselors. It has multiple applications for everything from marital counseling to executive development programs. Based on Carl Gustav Jung's theory of personality types, this simplified application of his complex theory attempts to measure personality dispositions and interests – the way people absorb information, decide, and communicate. It analyzes preferences to four dichotomies (extroversion/introversion, sensing/intuiting, thinking/feeling, judging/perceiving) which result in 16 personality types. The MBTI® comes in a variety of forms. Available through Consulting Psychologist Press (www.cpp.com and www.skillsone.com) and most colleges, universities, and testing centers.

- **16-Personality Factor Questionnaire (16PF):** This 185-question inventory analyzes adult personality in reference to 16 primary and eight secondary personality factors. Used for counseling, coaching, training, and self-assessment purposes to help individuals determine which occupations are best suited for them. Available through Pearson Assessments (www.pearson assessments.com).

Values

- **Career Beliefs Inventory (CBI):** Designed to assess an individual's beliefs about himself/herself and the work world. Includes a 96-item multiple-choice test. Available through Consulting Psychologists Press (www.cpp.com).

- **Minnesota Importance Questionnaire (MIQ):** Designed to measure an individual's vocational needs and values, which are important ingredients of work personality. Measures six vocational values (and 20 vocational needs that are the basis of these values): Achievement, Altruism, Comfort, Safety, Status, and Autonomy. Available through Vocational Psychology Research of the University of Minnesota (www.psych.umn.edu).

- **Survey of Interpersonal Values (SIV):** This 30-item inventory is designed to assess six interpersonal values as they relate to relationships with others as well as employment: support, conformity, recognition, independence, benevolence, and leadership. Available through NCS Pearson Reid London House (www.reidlondonhouse.com).

- **Temperament and Values Inventory:** This device is designed to assist individuals in identifying how they react to different activities and situations. In helping to determine job fit, this test measures what aspects of a job most motivates an individual.

- **O*NET Career Values Inventory:** Analyzes work values in reference to the major jobs outlined in the O*NET database of the U.S. Department of Labor. Available through JIST Publishing (http://jistworks.com).

Interests and Attitudes

- **Career Assessment Inventory™ – Enhanced Version (CAI-E):** Assesses the career interests of individuals re-entering the job market or making a career change. Includes a 370-item test using a 5-point Likert-type scale. Available through NCS Pearson (www.pearsonassessments.com).

- **Career Exploration Inventory:** Helps users assess their work, leisure, and learning interests in reference to 120 activity statements related to codes in the *Guide to Occupational Exploration*. Available through JIST Publishing (http://jistworks.com).

- **Career IQ and Interest Test (CIQIT):** Designed to help individuals identify jobs they do well and enjoy doing. Available through PRO-ED, Inc. (www.proedinc.com).

- **Guide to Occupational Exploration Interest Inventory:** Uses a multiple-choice and true/false testing format to explore career, education, and lifestyle options. Available through JIST Publishing (http://jistworks.com).

- **Harrington-O'Shea Career Decision-Making System:** Based on Holland's theory of vocational development, this device helps individuals to better understand their values and abilities for making career choices. Available through American Guidance Service (www.agsnet.com).

- **Jackson Vocational Interest Survey (JVIS):** Designed to assist counselors in evaluating the career interests of students and adults in transition. Available through Sigma Assessment Systems (http://jvis.com).

- **Job Search Attitude Inventory (JSAI):** Helps users better understand their motivation for conducting a job search. Available through JIST Publishing (http://jistworks.com).

- **Kuder Occupational Interest Survey:** This interest inventory is similar to the *Strong Interest Inventory*® and the six themes central to Holland's **Self-Directed Search**. It relates an individual's test results to six career clusters: Outdoor/Mechanical, Science/Technical, Arts/Communication, Social/Personal Services, Sales/Management, and Business Operations. It's especially useful in predicting job dissatisfaction. Available through National Career Assessment Services (www.kuder.com) and CareerLab (www.careerlab.com).

- **Leisure to Occupational Connection Search (LOCS):** Measures the relationship between vocational interests and leisure activities by examining 100 leisure activities to information on 250 jobs. Available through JIST Publishing (http://jistworks.com).

- **Leisure/Work Search Inventory:** Users respond to 96 leisure activity statements to assess how their leisure interests relate to employment opportunities. Available through JIST Publishing (http://jistworks.com).

- **Ohio Vocational Interest Survey:** This 253-item test assesses occupational and vocational interests in reference to three orientations – data, people, and things. Available through Harcourt Brace Educational Measurement (www.harcourt.com).

- **Self-Directed Search® (SDS):** One of the most widely used and adapted interest inventories in career counseling. Designed to assist individuals in making career choices based on an analysis of different orientations toward people, data, and things. It matches interests with six types (realistic, investigative, artistic, social, enterprising, and conventional) that are, in turn, related to different types of occupations that match these types. Used in helping determine how one's interests fit with various occupations. Influential in developing the assessment approach found in Richard Nelson Bolles's *What Color Is Your Parachute?* and *What Color Is Your Parachute Workbook*. Also available in other versions, such as *Self-Directed Search® Career Explorer (SDS® CE)* and *Self-Directed Search® Form R (SDS® Form R)*. Especially useful for students and others with little work experience who are interested in exploring job and career alternatives related to their interests. Available through Psychological Assessment Resources (www.parinc.com).

- **Strong Interest Inventory® :** Next to the *Myers-Briggs Type Indicator®* and the *Self-Directed Search®*, this remains one of the most popular assessment devices used by career counselors. Individuals respond to 317 multiple-choice items to determine their occupational interests according to six occupational themes, 25 interest scales, occupational scales, and personal style scales. Used extensively for career guidance, occupational decisions, employment placement, educational choices, and vocational rehabilitation programs. Available through Consulting Psychologist Press (www.cpp.com) and most schools, colleges, universities, and testing centers.

- **Vocational Interest Inventory:** Assists individuals with learning and other disabilities in making vocational decisions. Available through JIST Publishing (http://jistworks.com).

Skills, Behaviors, Aptitudes

- **Barriers to Employment Success Inventory:** Designed to assist the unemployed in identifying barriers to conducting a successful job search, this instrument includes 50 multiple-choice, short answer, and true/false items. Available through JIST Publishing (http://jistworks.com).

- **BRIGANCE® Diagnostic Employability Skills Inventory:** Helps identify basic employability skills and training needs. Available through Curriculum Associates, Inc. (www.curriculum associates.com).

- **Career Decision Scale:** Assists counselors in assessing a client's barriers to career decision-making. Available through Psychological Assessment Resources, Inc. (www.parinc.com).

- **FIRO-B® :** Used to assess an individual's interpersonal needs and how their behavior relates to the workplace. Measures "expressed" and "wanted" behaviors to help individuals better manage their behavior and increase productivity in the workplace. Available through Consulting Psychologists Press (www. cpp.com).

Multiple Indicators

- **APTICOM:** A popular vocational guidance and counseling instrument for assessing interests, aptitudes, and work-related math and language skills. Available through Vocational Research Institute (www.vri.org).

- **Armed Services Vocational Battery (ASVAB):** A 334-item test used to measure vocational interests and aptitudes related to military service. Available through the U.S. Department of Defense.

- **Assessment of Career Decision Making (ACDM):** Assists individuals in selecting a career compatible with their interests and abilities, Includes 96 true/false items. Available through Western Psychological Services (www.wpspublish.com).

- **The Birkman Method:** Used in many companies to both measure and enhance personal, team, and organizational effectiveness. Available online through Birkman International (www.birkman.com) and CareerLab (www.careerlab.com).

- **CAM Computerized One-Stop:** Designed to assess interests, aptitudes, attitudes, temperament, and learning styles of job applicants. Available through PESCO International (www.pesco.org).

- **Campbell™ Interest and Skill Survey (CISS®):** One of the most popular assessments devised for measuring interests and skills. Includes 320 items divided into 200 interest and 120 skill categories. Available through NCS Pearson (www.pearsonassessments.com).

- **Career Scope:** Includes 141 items that measure 12 interest and aptitude areas. Available through Vocational Research Institute (www.vri.org).

- **Key Educational Vocational Assessment System (KEVAS):** This device is designed to measure vocational interests and aptitudes. It matches aptitudes with specific jobs. Available through Key Education, Inc.

- **Vocational Interest, Temperament, and Aptitude System (VITAS):** A vocational guidance instrument used for assessing aptitudes, vocational interests, and work-related temperaments of the special needs populations. Available through Vocational Research Institute (www.vri.org).

For a quick review of these and many other assessment tests, see the following reference volumes:

Career Tests, Louis Janda (Avon, MA: Adams Media)

The ETS Test Collection Catalog (New York: Oryx Press)

Mental Measures Yearbook (Lincoln, NE: University of Nebraska Press)

Tests, Taddy Maddox, ed. (Austin, TX: Pro-Ed)

What Type Am I?, Renee Baron (New York: Penguin Books)

Computerized Assessment Programs

While some of the various inventories outlined above are available in computer programs, others are strictly computerized career guidance programs available for Windows and the Internet. Most are expensive licensed programs that can be found at career centers in high schools, colleges, one-stops, libraries, and community-based organizations. Two of the most popular and comprehensive such programs are:

- **SIGI Plus** (System of Interactive Guidance and Information): Designed to help individuals make better education and career decisions. Helps clarify work values and then relates those values to specific occupations which also relate to the user's interests and work skills. Assists students in identifying education and training paths appropriate for their particular mix of values, interests, and skills. Available through Valpar International Corporation (www. valparint.com).

- **Discover:** Available in both Windows CD and Internet versions, this program also helps individuals make better educational and career choices through an analysis of their values, interests, and abilities. Users identify their strengths and needs and then relate them to specific occupational and educational alternatives. Includes a comprehensive database of occupations, college majors, schools and training institutions, financial aid/scholarships, and military options. Available through ACT (www.act.org).

These programs require users to answer a series of questions which are analyzed and then related to different occupations that best match the individual's interests, skills, and values profile.

Online Assessments

Within the past few years, several companies have developed online assessment devices which you can quickly access via the Internet 24 hours a day in the comfort of your home or office. Some tests are self-scoring and free of charge while others require interacting with a fee-based certified career counselor or testing expert. SkillsOne (www.skillsone.com), for example, is operated by the producers of the *Myers-Briggs Type Indicator®* and *Strong Interest Inventory®* – Consulting Psychologists Press. CareerLab (www.careerlab.com) offers one of the largest batteries of well respected assessment tools: *Campbell Interest and Skills Survey, Strong Interest Inventory®, Myers-Briggs Type Indicator®, 16-Personality Factors Profile, FIRO-B®, California Psychological Inventory (CPI), The Birkman Method*, and *Campbell Leadership Index*. The following seven websites are well worth exploring for both free and fee-based online assessments tools:

- **SkillsOne**   www.skillsone.com
  (Consulting Psychologists Press)   www.cpp-db.com
- **CareerLab.com**   www.careerlab.com
- **Self-Directed Search®**   www.self-directed-search.com
- **Personality Online**   www.personalityonline.com
- **Keirsey Character Sorter**   www.keirsey.com
- **MAPP™**   www.assessment.com
- **PersonalityType**   www.personalitytype.com

These 18 additional sites also include a wealth of related assessment devices that you can access online:

- **Analyze My Career**   www.analyzemycareer.com
- **Birkman Method**   www.birkman.com
- **Career Key**   www.careerkey.org/english
- **CareerLeader™**   www.careerleader
- **CareerPlanner.com**   www.careerplanner.com
- **CareerPerfect.com**   www.careerperfect.com

- Careers By Design®   www.careers-by-design.com
- College Board   www.myroad.com
- Enneagram   www.ennea.com
- Fortune.com   www.fortune.com/fortune/
                             careers
- Humanmetrics   www.humanmetrics.com
- Jackson Vocational
  Interest Inventory   www.jvis.com
- My Future   www.myfuture.com
- People Management
  International   www.sima-pmi.com
- Personality and IQ Tests   www.davideck.com
- Profiler   www.profiler.com
- QueenDom   www.queendom.com
- Tests on the Web   www.2h.com
- Tickle   www.web.tickle.com/tests/
                             career.jsp

Doing It Right From the Very Start

As we will see in Chapter 8, identifying your motivated abilities and skills is one of the very first things you should do in your job search – before writing your resume, conducting research, networking, and responding to job opportunities.

> *Based on your self-assessment work, you will be able to clearly communicate to employers what it is you will most likely do for them.*

The sooner you discover what it is you do well and enjoy doing, the more focused, energetic, fun, and fascinating will be your job search. You will approach the job world and connect with the right people from a whole new and positive perspective. You will be able to clearly communicate to employers what it is you will most likely do for them because you have documented your accomplishments through self-assessment. Unlike other job seekers who make the mistake of not knowing their abilities and skills, and thereby have difficulty specifying an objective, you should stand out from the crowd because of your employer-centered approach. Employers will immediately know what you can do for them. Better still, they will want to invite you to an interview to learn more about your accomplishments in reference to their needs. At the interview, you will have an important story to share with them about who you are and what you will most likely do for them. When they say *"You're hired!"* it's probably because you convinced them that you had the right combination of motivated abilities and skills to do the job.

5

Develop a Vision of Your Future Job and Career

KNOWING WHAT YOU WANT to do in the future will be based in part on a vision of what jobs are available for someone with your interests, skills, and abilities. Perhaps you are already working in an information technology field where more and more jobs are being offshored to cheap labor markets abroad; your job could soon disappear or your wages decline significantly. If you are contemplating changing careers by pursuing an MBA degree but discover few jobs will be available for MBAs when you graduate in two years, you may decide to forego spending the time and money to pursue an MBA degree. At the same time, you may want to consider becoming a paralegal, dental hygienist, or teacher, because you learn these are some of the hottest and most satisfying career fields in the decade ahead. Whatever your choices, you'll want to explore different jobs and careers based upon the latest information about future job prospects combined with an understanding of your interests and skills.

Jobs With a Bright Future

Where are the jobs, and how do I get one? These are the first two questions most people ask when seeking employment. They're interesting questions if you're trying to fit into a job rather than find a job fit for you.

Two other equally important questions should precede these traditional questions:

"What jobs most interest me?"

"What jobs would be the best fit for me?"

For the nature of jobs is changing rapidly in response to (1) the application of new technology to the workplace, (2) increased worker productivity, (3) the demand for more consumer goods and services, and (4) changes in the global economy. Today's job seeker needs answers to the "what," "where," and "how" of jobs for today and tomorrow in order to determine how they might best fit into the larger employment picture.

Many jobs in the decade ahead will look very different from those of yesterday. Indeed, if we project present trends into the future and believe what futurists tell us about emerging new careers, the next two decades will offer unprecedented and exciting opportunities for individuals who are equipped with the necessary skills to pursue their dreams.

But such changes and opportunities have costs. The change in jobs and occupations will be so rapid that skills learned today may become obsolete in another five to 10 years. Therefore, knowing what the jobs are becomes a prerequisite to knowing how to prepare for them, find them, and change them in the future.

> *If you wish to identify a growing career field to plan your own career, do so only after you identify your interests, skills, and abilities.*

A few words of caution are in order on how you should and should not use the information in this chapter. If you wish to identify a growing career field to plan your own career, do so only **after** you identify your values, interests, skills, and motivated abilities – the subjects of Chapters 5, 6, 7, and 8. You need to know if that career field is appropriate for you and vice versa. Furthermore, you need to determine if you have the proper skills or aptitude and interests to acquire the necessary skills. The next step is to acquire the training before conducting a job search. Only then should you seriously consider pursuing what appears to be a growing field. At the same time, during a period of turbulent change, occupational profiles may become quickly outdated. Training requirements change, and thus individuals encounter greater uncertainty in career choices.

Let's examine projected job trends in the decade ahead in order to get a better idea of where your career interests might lie in terms of specific occupations and jobs. In so doing, you'll have a better idea of what you will most likely do well and enjoy doing in the future.

Expect Continuing Job Growth

The growth in jobs has been steady during the past three to four decades. From 1955 to 1980, for example, the number of jobs increased from 68.7 to 105.6 million. This represented an average annual increase of about 1.5 million new jobs. During the 1970s the number of jobs increased by over 2 million per year. And between the years 1983 and 1994 the number of jobs increased by 24.6 million, a strong growth rate of 24 percent over an 11-year period or over 2 million new jobs each year. Between 1995 and 1999, jobs grew by over 2 million each year. By the year 2012 employment is expected to increase from 144 million in 2002 to 165 million in 2012, or by 14.8 percent.

Highlighting these patterns of job growth are 16 forecasts, based on U.S. Department of Labor data and projections and other recent analyses, which represent the recent confluence of demographic, economic, and technological changes in society:

1. Growth of the labor force slows.

The growth in the labor force will slow to 162.3 million by the year 2012 – a 17.4 percent increase from the year 2002. The U.S. population is expected to increase by 24 million over the 2002-12 period, which is slower than in the two previous decades.

2. The labor force will be racially and ethnically more diverse.

The U.S. workforce will be more diverse by 2012. White, non-Hispanic persons will continue to make up a decreasing share of the labor force, falling from 71.3 percent in 2002 to 65.5 percent in 2012. White, non-Hispanics will remain the largest group in the labor force in 2012. Hispanics are projected to account for an increasing share of the labor force by 2012, growing from 12.4 to 14.7 percent. By 2012, Hispanics will constitute a larger proportion of the labor force than will blacks, whose share will grow from 11.4 percent to 12.2 percent. Asians will continue to be the fastest growing of the four labor force groups.

3. Fewer young people will enter the job market.

The youth labor force, aged 16 to 24, is expected to slightly decrease its share of the labor force to 15 percent by 2012 or just over 24 million. Businesses depending on this age group for students, recruits, customers, and part-time workers – especially colleges, the armed forces, eating and drinking establishments, and retail stores – must draw from a smaller pool of young people. Competition among young people for entry-level jobs will decline accordingly.

4. The workforce will continue to gray as it becomes older.

The number of workers 55 and older will increase substantially by the year 2012. This group is expected to increase from 14.3 percent to 19.1 percent of the labor force between 2002 and 2012, due to the aging of the baby-boom generation.

5. Women will continue to enter the labor force in growing numbers.

The male labor force is projected to grow by 10 percent from 2002 to 2012, compared with 14.3 percent for women. Men's share of the labor force is expected to decrease from 53.5 to 52.5 percent, while women's share is expected to increase from 46.5 to 47.5 percent. By the year 2012, four out of five women ages 25-54 will be in the labor force.

6. Education requirements for most new jobs will rise.

Most new jobs will require strong basic education skills, such as reading, writing, oral communication, and math. Many of these jobs will include important high-tech components, which will require specialized education and training as well as the demonstrated ability to learn and acquire nontraditional education and training to continuously re-tool.

7. **The fastest growing occupations will be in executive, managerial, professional, and technical fields – all requiring the highest levels of education and skill.**

Three-quarters of the fastest growing occupational groups will be executive, administrative, and managerial; professional specialty; and technicians and related support occupations – occupations that require the highest levels of education and skill. Few opportunities will be available for high school dropouts or those who cannot read or follow directions. A combination of greater emphasis on productivity in the workplace, increased automation, technological advances, innovations, and changes in consumer demands will decrease the need for workers with little formal education and few skills – helpers, laborers, assemblers, machine operators.

8. **Employment will continue to increase for most occupations.**

As the population continues to grow and become more middle-aged and affluent, demands for more services will increase accordingly. Except in the cases of agriculture, mining, and traditional manufacturing, the past decade has seen a steady to significant job growth in all occupations. Over 21 million jobs will be added to the U.S. economy between the years 2002 and 2012. However, new jobs will be unevenly distributed across major industrial and occupational groups due to the restructuring of the economy and the increased education and training requirements for most jobs. Professional and related occupations will grow the fastest and add more new jobs than any other major occupational group.

9. **The greatest growth in jobs will take place in service industries and occupations as the long-term shift from goods-producing to service-providing employment continues.**

Over 90 percent of all new jobs in the 1990s were in the service-producing industries with services such as legal, business (advertising, accounting, and computer support), and healthcare leading the way. The number of jobs in the service-producing industries is expected to account for approximately 20.8 million of the 21.6 million new wage and salary jobs generated over the 2002-2012 period.

10. Education and health services will add more jobs than any other industry supersector.

This industry supersector is expected to grow by 31.8 percent during the 2002-2012 period. About one out of every four new jobs created in the U.S. economy will be in either the healthcare and social assistance or private education services sector.

11. Government employment will increase at different rates for different levels of government as well as for governmental units in different regions of the country.

Between 2002 and 2012, government employment, including public education and hospitals, is expected to increase by 11.8 percent, form 21.5 million to 24 million jobs. Growth in government employment will be fueled by growth in state and local educational services and the shift of responsibilities from the federal government to the state and local governments. Local government education services is projected to increase 17.5 percent, adding over 1.3 million jobs. State government education services also are projected to grow 17.5 percent, adding 388,000 jobs. Federal government employment, including the Postal Service, is expected to increase by less than 1 percent as the federal government continues to contract out many government jobs to private companies.

12. Employment growth in education will be incremental.

Private educational services will grow by 28.7 percent and add 759,000 new jobs through 2012. Rising student enrollments at all levels of education will create demand for educational services. Job opportunities should increase for teachers, teacher aides, counselors, and administrative staff.

13. Jobs in manufacturing will continue to decline.

Manufacturing jobs are expected to decline by 1 percent, or 157,000 jobs, in the period 2002-2012. Most of the decline will affect production jobs; professional, technical, and managerial positions in manufacturing will increase. Production job declines will be due to productivity gains achieved through automation and improved management as well as the closing of less efficient plants. However, employment in plastics and rubber products manufacturing and machinery manufacturing is expected to grow by 138,000 and 120,000 jobs, respectively. Due to an aging population and increasing life expectancies, pharmaceutical manufacturing is expected to grow by 23.2 percent and add 68,000 jobs through 2012.

14. Employment in agriculture, forestry, fishing, and mining jobs will continue to decline.

Employment in agriculture, forestry, and fishing is expected to decline by 2 percent from 2002 to 2012, due to advancements in technology. The only supersector expected to grow is support activities for agriculture and forestry, which includes farm labor contractors and farm management services. This industry is expected to grow by 18.4 percent and add 17,000 new jobs. Strong growth will take place in agricultural services industries, especially landscape, horticultural, and farm management services. Much of the self-employment decline in agriculture will be due to the closing of lucrative export markets as the productivity of agriculture abroad improves and new hybrid crops are introduced from genetic engineering breakthroughs to solve many of the world's food problems.

15. Glamorous new occupations, responding to new technological developments and consumer demands, will offer exciting new opportunities for job seekers who are well educated and skilled in the jobs of tomorrow.

New occupations, created through a combination of technological innovations and new service demands, will provide excellent career opportunities for those who possess the necessary skills and drive to succeed in the decade ahead. New occupations with such names

as bionic-electronic technician, holographic inspector, cryonics technician, and aquaculturist will enter our occupational vocabulary
during the coming decade.

16. **The hottest career fields for the first decade of the 21st
century will be in science, engineering, computer technology, and health services.**

Look for these jobs to be the highest demand and highest paying
jobs for the coming decade: biological scientist, physician, mechanical engineer, chemical engineer, computer scientist, computer engineer, materials engineer, medical technologist. Demand also will
be high for these less well paid jobs: special education teachers,
personal and home care aides, home health aides, and physical
therapists.

Growing and Declining Occupations

The U.S. Department of Labor divides occupations into 16 broad groups
based on the Standard Occupational Classification, the classification
system used by all government agencies for collecting occupational
information:

- Executive, administrative, and managerial occupations
- Engineers, scientists, and related occupations
- Social science, social service, and related occupations
- Teachers, librarians, and counselors
- Health-related occupations
- Writers, artists, and entertainers
- Technologists and technicians
- Marketing and sales occupations
- Administrative support occupations, including clerical
- Service occupations
- Agricultural and forestry occupations
- Mechanics and repairers
- Construction occupations
- Production occupations
- Transportation and material moving occupations
- Handlers, equipment cleaners, helpers, and laborers

Every two years the department's Bureau of Labor Statistics updates its employment outlook for the coming decade and publishes the results in the November issue of the ***Monthly Labor Review*** as well as the latest edition of the biannual ***Occupational Outlook Handbook***. For the latest statistics and projections relating to several tables presented in this chapter, please visit the website of the Bureau of Labor Statistics: http://stats.bls.gov. You also can access online the complete text of the popular ***Occupational Outlook Handbook***:

www.bls.gov/oco

Assuming a moderate rate of economic growth in the decade ahead – not boom-and-bust cycles – the U.S. Department of Labor projects an average growth rate of nearly 15 percent for all occupations in the coming decade. Technical and service occupations will grow the fastest:

Fastest Growing Occupations, 2002-2012
(Numbers in thousands of jobs)

Occupational Title	Employment 2002	Employment 2012	Percent Change	Postsecondary Education or Training
▪ Medical assistants [3]	365	579	59	Moderate-term on-the-job training
▪ Network systems and data communications analysts [1]	186	292	57	Bachelor's degree
▪ Physician assistants [3]	63	94	49	Bachelor's degree
▪ Social and human service assistants [3]	305	454	49	Moderate-term on-the-job training
▪ Home health aides [4]	580	859	48	Short-term on-the-job training
▪ Medical records and health information technicians [3]	147	216	47	Associate degree
▪ Physical therapist aides [3]	37	54	46	Short-term on-the-job training
▪ Computer software engineers, applications [1]	394	573	46	Bachelor's degree
▪ Computer software engineers [1]	281	409	45	Bachelor's degree
▪ Physical therapist assistants [2]	50	73	45	Associate degree

▪ Fitness trainers and aerobics instructors [3]	183	264	44	Postsecondary vocational award
▪ Database administrators [1]	110	159	44	Bachelor's degree
▪ Veterinary technologists and technicians [3]	53	76	44	Associate degree
▪ Hazardous materials removal workers [2]	38	54	43	Moderate-term on-the-job training
▪ Dental hygienists [1]	148	212	43	Associate degree
▪ Occupational therapist aides [3]	8	12	43	Short-term on-the-job training
▪ Dental assistants [3]	266	379	42	Moderate-term on-the-job training
▪ Personal and home care aides [4]	608	854	40	Short-term on-the-job training
▪ Self-enrichment education teachers [2]	200	281	40	Work experience in a related occupation
▪ Computer systems analysts [1]	468	653	39	Bachelor's degree
▪ Occupational therapist assistants [2]	18	26	39	Associate degree
▪ Environmental engineers [1]	47	65	38	Bachelor's degree
▪ Postsecondary teachers [1]	1,581	1,284	38	Doctoral degree
▪ Network and computer systems administrators [1]	251	345	37	Bachelor's degree
▪ Environmental science and protection technicians, including health [2]	28	38	37	Associate degree
▪ Preschool teachers, except special education [4]	424	577	36	Postsecondary vocational award
▪ Computer and information systems managers [1]	284	387	36	Bachelor's or higher degree, plus work experience
▪ Physical therapists [1]	137	185	35	Master's degree
▪ Occupational therapists [1]	82	110	35	Bachelor's degree
▪ Respiratory therapists [2]	86	116	35	Associate degree

[1] Very high average annual earnings ($42,820 and over)
[2] High average annual earnings ($27,500 to $41,780)
[3] Low average annual earnings ($19,710 to $27,380)
[4] Very low average annual earnings (up to $19,600)

Occupations With the Largest Job Growth, 2002-2012
(Numbers in thousands of jobs)

Occupational Title	Employment 2002	2012	Percent Change	Postsecondary Education or Training
■ Registered nurses [1]	2,284	2,908	27	Associate degree
■ Postsecondary teachers [1]	1,581	2,184	38	Doctoral degree
■ Retail salespersons [4]	4,076	4,672	15	Short-term on-the-job training
■ Customer service representatives [3]	1,894	2,354	24	Moderate-term on-the-job training
■ Combined food preparation and service workers, including fast food [3]	1,990	2,444	23	Short-term on-the-job training
■ Cashiers, except gaming [4]	3,432	2,886	13	Short-term on-the-job training
■ Janitors and cleaners, except maids and housekeeping cleaners [4]	2,267	2,681	18	Short-term on-the-job training
■ General and operations managers [1]	2,049	2,425	18	Bachelor's or higher degree + experience
■ Waiters and waitresses [4]	2,097	2,464	18	Short-term on-the-job training
■ Nursing aides, orderlies, and attendants [3]	1,375	1,718	25	Short-term on-the-job training
■ Truck drivers, heavy and tractor-trailer [2]	1,767	2,104	19	Moderate-term on-the-job training
■ Receptionists and information clerks [3]	1,100	1,425	29	Short-term on-the-job training
■ Security guards [4]	995	1,313	32	Short-term on-the-job training
■ Office clerks, general [3]	2,991	3,301	10	Short-term on-the-job training
■ Teacher assistants [4]	1,277	1,571	23	Short-term on-the-job training
■ Sales representative, wholesale and manufacturing, except technical and scientific products [1]	1,459	1,738	19	Moderate-term on-the-job training
■ Home health aides [4]	580	859	48	Short-term on-the-job training

▪ Personal and home care aides [4]	608	854	40	Short-term on-the-job training
▪ Truck drivers, light or delivery services [3]	1,022	1,259	23	Short-term on-the-job training
▪ Landscaping and groundskeeping workers [3]	1,074	1,311	22	Short-term on-the-job training
▪ Elementary school teachers, except special education [2]	1,467	1,690	15	Bachelor's degree
▪ Medical assistants [3]	365	579	59	Moderate-term on-the-job training
▪ Maintenance and repair workers, general [2]	1,266	1,472	16	Moderate-term on-the-job training
▪ Accountants and auditors [1]	1,055	1,261	19	Bachelor's degree
▪ Computer systems analysts [1]	468	653	39	Bachelor's degree
▪ Secondary school teachers, except special and vocational education [1]	988	1,167	18	Bachelor's degree
▪ Computer software engineers [1]	394	573	46	Bachelor's degree
▪ Management analysis [1]	577	753	30	Bachelor's or higher degree, plus work experience
▪ Food preparation workers [4]	850	1,022	20	Short-term on-the-job training
▪ First-line supervisors/ manager of retail sales workers [2]	1,798	1,962	9	Work experience in a related occupation

[1] Very high average annual earnings ($42,820 and over)
[2] High average annual earnings ($27,500 to $41,780)
[3] Low average annual earnings ($19,710 to $27,380)
[4] Very low average annual earnings (up to $19,600)

Fastest Growing Industries, 2002-2012
(Numbers in thousands of jobs)

Industry Description	Jobs		Percent Change	Average annual rate of change
	2002	2012		
▪ Software publishers	256.0	429.7	173.7	5.3
▪ Management, scientific, and technical consulting services	731.8	1,137.4	405.6	4.5

■ Community care facilities for the elderly and residential care facilities	695.3	1,077.6	382.3	4.5
■ Computer systems design and related services	1,162.7	1,797.7	635.0	4.5
■ Employment services	3,248.8	5,012.3	1,763.5	4.4
■ Individual, family, community, and vocational rehabilitation services	1,238.8	1,866.6	597.3	3.9
■ Ambulatory health care services except offices of health practitioners	1,443.6	2,113.4	669.8	3.9
■ Water, sewage, and other systems	48.5	71.0	22.5	3.9
■ Internet services, data processing, and other information services	528.8	773.1	244.3	3.9
■ Child day care services	734.2	1,050.3	316.1	3.6

20 Jobs With High Median Earnings and a Significant Number of Job Openings, 2002-2012

Occupation	Average Annual Projected Job Openings, 2002-2012	Median Earnings 2002
■ Registered nurses	110,119	$48,090
■ Postsecondary teachers	95,980	$49,090
■ General and operations managers	76,245	$68,210
■ Sales representatives, wholesale and manufacturing, except technical and scientific products	66,239	$42,730
■ Truck drivers, heavy and tractor-trailer	62,517	$33,210
■ Elementary school teachers, except special education	54,701	$41,780
■ First-line supervisors or managers of retail sales workers	48,645	$29,700
■ Secondary school teachers, except special education	45,761	$43,950
■ General maintenance and repair workers	44,978	$29,370

- Executive secretaries and
  administrative assistants 42,444 $33,410
- First-line supervisors or managers
  of office and administrative
  support workers 40,909 $38,820
- Accountants and auditors 40,465 $47,000
- Carpenters 31,917 $34,190
- Automotive service technicians
  and mechanics 41,887 $30,590
- Police and sheriff's patrol officers 31,290 $42,270
- Licensed practical and licensed
  vocational nurses 29,480 $31,440
- Electricians 28,485 $41,390
- Management analysts 25,470 $60,340
- Computer systems analysts 23,735 $62,890
- Special education teachers 23,297 $43,450

Certain patterns are clearly evident from the U.S. Department of Labor's employment projections for the coming decade:

1. The hot occupational fields are in healthcare and computers and involve increased technical education and training on an ongoing basis.

2. Education is closely associated with earnings – the higher the education, the higher the average annual earnings.

3. Many of the fastest growing jobs require short- or moderate-term education.

4. Two-year associate degrees in several medical-related fields offer some of the best paying jobs.

5. Nearly 50 percent of the fastest growing jobs that generate relatively high median earnings, such as carpenters, truck drivers, repair workers, and auto mechanics, do not require a four-year degree.

Survey Today's "Best" Jobs

The fastest growing occupational fields are not necessarily the best ones to enter. The best job and career for you will depend on your particular mix of skills, interests, and work and lifestyle values. Money, for example, is only one of many determiners of whether or not a job and career are particularly desirable. A job may pay a great deal of money, but it also may be very stressful and insecure, or it is found in an undesirable location. The "best" job for you will be one you find very rewarding in terms of your own criteria and priorities.

Periodically some observers of the labor market attempt to identify what are the best, the worst, the hottest, the most lucrative, or the most promising jobs and careers of the decade. One of the most ambitious attempts to assemble a list of the "best" jobs in America is presented in Les Krantz's *Jobs Rated Almanac*. Similar in methodology to *Places Rated Almanac* for identifying the best places to live in America, the latest edition (2002) of this book evaluates and ranks 250 jobs in terms of six primary "job quality" criteria: income, stress, physical demands, environment, outlook, and security. According to this analysis, the 25 highest ranking ("best") jobs by accumulated score of these criteria are:

The Best Jobs in America

Job title	Overall rank
▪ Biologist	1
▪ Actuary	2
▪ Financial planner	3
▪ Computer system analyst	4
▪ Accountant	5
▪ Software engineer	6
▪ Meteorologist	7
▪ Paralegal assistant	8
▪ Statistician	9
▪ Astronomer	10
▪ Mathematician	11
▪ Parole officer	12
▪ Hospital administrator	13
▪ Architectural drafter	14
▪ Physiologist	15
▪ Dietician	16
▪ Website manager	17
▪ Physicist	18

- Audiologist   19
- Agency director (nonprofit)   20
- Industrial designer   21
- Chemist   22
- Medical laboratory technician   23
- Archeologist   24
- Economist   25

The 20 worst jobs, or those that rank at the very bottom of the list of 250, include the following:

The Worst Jobs in America

Job title	Overall rank
■ Fisherman	250
■ Roustabout	249
■ Lumberjack	248
■ Cowboy	247
■ Ironworker	246
■ Garbage collector	245
■ Construction worker (laborer)	244
■ Taxi driver	243
■ Stevedore	242
■ Roofer	240
■ Dancer	239
■ Firefighter	238
■ Dairy Farmer	237
■ Seaman	236
■ Farmer	235
■ Boilermaker	234
■ Carpenter	234
■ Sheet metal worker	232
■ Butcher	231

For the relative rankings of all 250 jobs as well as the ratings of each job on individual criterion, consult the latest edition of the *Jobs Rated Almanac*, which should be available in your local library or bookstore.

One of the most recent examinations of the best jobs in the decade ahead – those offering high pay, fast growth, and the most new jobs – is found in Ferguson's latest edition of *25 Jobs That Have It All* (New York: Facts on File). They identify these 25 jobs as the top ones:

- Advertising account executive
- Business manager
- College professor

- Computer network administrator
- Computer systems programmers/analyst
- Database specialist
- Dental hygienist
- Graphic designer
- Health care manager
- Management analyst and consultant
- Occupational therapist
- Paralegal
- Pharmacy technician
- Physician assistant
- Police officer
- Public relations specialist
- Registered nurse
- Secondary school teacher
- Software designer
- Software engineer
- Special education teacher
- Speech-language pathologist and audiologist
- Technical support specialist
- Writer and editor

Anticipate Exciting New Occupations

In the early 1980s the auto and related industries – steel, rubber, glass, aluminum, railroads, and auto dealers – accounted for one-fifth of all employment in the United States. Today that percentage continues to decline as service occupations further dominate America's occupational structure.

New occupations for the decade ahead will center around information, energy, high-tech, healthcare, and financial industries. They promise to create a new occupational structure and vocabulary relating to computers, the Internet, robotics, biotechnology, lasers, and fiber optics. By 1999, for example, the Internet reportedly was responsible for 1.3 million new jobs within a four-year period that generated more than $300 billion in business. And as these fields begin to apply new technologies to developing new innovations, they in turn will generate other new occupations in the 21st century. While most new occupations are not major growth fields

– because they do not initially generate a large number of new jobs – they will present individuals with fascinating new opportunities to become leaders in pioneering new fields and industries.

Futurists agree that most new occupations in the coming decade will have two dominant characteristics:

- **They will generate fewer new jobs** in comparison to the overall growth of jobs in hundreds of more traditional service fields, such as sales workers, office clerks, truck drivers, and janitors.

- **They require a high level of education and skills** for entry into the fields as well as continuing training and retraining as each field transforms itself into additional growth fields.

If you plan to pursue an emerging occupation, expect to first acquire highly specialized skills which may require years of higher education and training.

Job Trends and Your Choices

Most growth industries and occupations require skills training and experience. Moving into one of these fields will require knowledge of job qualifications, the nature of the work, and sources of employment. Fortunately, the U.S. Department of Labor publishes several useful sources of information available in most libraries to help you. These include the *O*NET Dictionary of Occupational Titles*, which identifies over 1,100 job titles (reduced from 13,000 titles found in the old *Dictionary of Occupational Titles*). The *Occupational Outlook Handbook* provides an overview of current labor market conditions and projections, as well as discusses nearly 250 occupations that account for 107 million jobs, or 87 percent of the nation's total jobs, according to several useful informational categories: nature of work; working conditions; employment; training, other qualifications, and achievement; job outlook; earnings; related occupations; and sources of additional information. Our own *America's Top 100 Jobs for People Without a Four-Year Degree* and *America's Top Jobs for People Re-Entering the Workforce* identify numerous jobs for people contemplating job or career changes.

During the past eight years, the U.S. Department of Labor overhauled its traditional job classification system which was based on an analysis of the U.S. job market of the 1960s, 1970s, and 1980s. This system had generated over 13,000 job titles as outlined in the ***Dictionary of Occupational Titles*** and numerous related publications. Known as the O*NET project (The Occupational Information Network), this new occupational classification system more accurately reflects the structure of today's new job market; it condenses the 13,000+ job titles into over 1,100 job titles. The new system is being gradually introduced into career education to replace the job classification system that has defined most jobs in the U.S. during the past four decades.

Anyone seeking to enter the job market or change careers should initially consult the U.S. Department of Labor publications as well as access information on the new O*NET (www.onetcenter.org). The Department of Labor only makes this data available online (http://online.onetcenter.org). A commercial version of this system, published in book form, also is available. You should be able to find it in your local library. If not, the ***O*NET Dictionary of Occupational Titles*** can be ordered from Impact Publications by completing the form at the end of this book or through Impact's online bookstore: www.impactpublications.com.

However, remember that labor market statistics are for industries and occupations **as a whole**. They tell you little about the shift in employment emphasis **within the industry,** and nothing about the outlook of particular jobs for you, **the individual**. For example, employment in agriculture was projected to decline by 14 percent between 1985 and 2000, but the decline consisted of an important shift in employment emphasis within the industry: there would be 500,000 fewer self-employed workers but 150,000 more wage and salary earners in the service end of agriculture. The employment statistics also assume a steady state of economic growth with consumers having more and more disposable income to stimulate a wide variety of service and trade industries.

Therefore, be careful in how you interpret and use this information in making your own job and career decisions. If, for example, you want to become a college teacher, and the data tells you there will be a 10-percent decline in this occupation during the next 10 years, this does not mean you would not find employment, as well as advance, in this field. It merely means that, on the whole, competition may be keen for these jobs, and that future advancement and mobility in this occupation may not be very good – **on the whole**. At the same time, there may be numerous job opportunities available in a declining occupational field as many individuals abandon the field for more attractive occupations. In fact, you may do much better in this declining occupation than in a growing field depending on your interests, motivations, abilities, job search savvy, and level of competition. And if the decade ahead experiences more boom-and-bust cycles, expect most of these U.S. Department of Labor statistics and projections to be invalid for the economic realities of this decade.

Use this industrial and occupational data to expand your awareness of various job and career options. By no means should you make critical education, training, and occupational choices based upon this information alone. Such choices require additional types of information – subjects of the next three chapters – about you, the individual. If identified and used properly, this information will help clarify exactly what you want to do in the future in terms of specific jobs and careers.

6

Your Skills and Abilities

T AKING SELF-ASSESSMENT TESTS and surveying job options are good starting points for identifying what you want to do with the rest of your life. However, you need to generate more substantive information about yourself before you are ready to formulate an objective and launch a well-organized and targeted job search. You can do this by completing several self-directed exercises that focus on your strengths – those things you especially do well. In this chapter we examine the most basic career building blocks – your skills and abilities.

Communicating and Transferring Skills

We live in a skills-based society where individuals market their skills to employers in exchange for money, position, and power. The ease by which they change jobs and careers is directly related to their ability to communicate their skills to employers and then transfer them to new work settings.

To best position yourself in the job markets of today and tomorrow, you should pay particular attention to refining your present skills as well as acquiring new and more marketable skills.

Your Skills

But before you can refine your skills or acquire additional skills, you need to know what skills you presently possess. Unfortunately, few people can identify and talk about their skills even though they possess hundreds of skills which they use on a regular basis. This becomes a real problem when they must write a resume or go to a job interview. Since employers want to know about your specific abilities and skills, you must learn to both identify and communicate your skills to employers. You should be able to explain what it is you do well and give examples relevant to employers' needs.

What skills do you already have to offer employers? If you have just completed an educational program, the skills you have to offer are most likely related to the subject matter you studied. If you are changing jobs or careers, the skills you wish to communicate to employers will be those things you already have demonstrated you can do in specific jobs.

As we noted earlier, the skills required for **finding a job** are no substitute for the skills necessary for **doing the job**. Learning new skills requires a major investment of time, money, and effort. Nonetheless, the long-term pay-off should more than justify the initial costs. Indeed, research continues to show that well selected education and training provide the best returns on individual and societal investment.

Types of Skills

Most people possess two types of skills that define their accomplishments and strengths as well as enable them to enter and advance within the job market: work-content skills and functional skills. You need to acquaint yourself with these skills before communicating them to employers. These skills become the key language for communicating your qualifications to employers through your resumes and letters as well as in interviews. They can be expressed in the form of both verbs and nouns – an important distinction that differentiates a conventional paper resume from an electronic scannable resume.

We assume you have already acquired certain **work-content skills** necessary to function effectively in today's job market. These "hard skills" are easy to recognize since they are often identified as "qualifications" for specific jobs; they are the subject of most educational and training programs. Work-content skills tend to be technical and job-specific in nature. Examples of such skills include proficiency in designing Web pages, programming computers, teaching accounting, or operating an X-ray machine. They may require formal training, are associated with specific trades or professions, and are used only in certain job and career settings. One uses a separate skills vocabulary, jargon, and subject matter for specifying technical qualifications of individuals entering and advancing in an occupation. While these skills do not transfer well from one occupation to another, they are critical for entering and advancing within certain occupations.

At the same time, you possess numerous **functional/transferable skills** employers readily seek along with your work-content skills. These "soft skills" are associated with numerous job settings, are mainly acquired through experience rather than formal training, and can be communicated through a general vocabulary. Functional/transferable skills are less easy to recognize since

> *Functional skills can be transferred from one job or career to another.*

they tend to be linked to certain **personal characteristics** (energetic, intelligent, likable) and the ability to **deal with processes** (communicating, problem-solving, motivating) rather than **do things** (programming a computer, building a house, repairing air-conditioners). While most people have only a few work-content skills, they may have numerous – as many as 300 – functional/transferable skills. These skills enable job seekers to more easily change jobs. But you must first be aware of your functional skills before you can relate them to the job market.

Most people view the world of work in traditional occupational job skill terms. This is a **structural view** of occupational realities. Occupational fields are seen as consisting of separate and distinct jobs which, in turn, require specific work-content skills. From this perspective, occupations and jobs are relatively self-contained entities. Social work, for example, is seen as being different from paralegal work; social workers, therefore, are not "qualified" to seek paralegal work.

On the other hand, a **functional view** of occupations and jobs emphasizes the similarity of job characteristics as well as common linkages between different occupations. Although the structure of occupations and jobs may differ, they have similar functions. They involve working with people, data, processes, and objects. If you work with people, data, processes, and objects in one occupation, you can transfer that experience to other occupations which have similar functions. Once you understand how your skills relate to the functions as well as investigate the structure of different occupations, you should be prepared to make job changes from one occupational field to another. Whether you possess the necessary work-content skills to qualify for entry into the other occupational field is another question altogether.

The skills we identify and help you organize in this chapter are the functional skills career counselors normally emphasize when advising clients to assess their **strengths**. In contrast to work-content skills, functional skills can be transferred from one job or career to another. They enable individuals to make some job and career changes without acquiring additional education and training. They constitute an important bridge for moving from one occupation to another.

> *Your goal should be to find a job that is fit for you rather than one you think you might be able to fit into.*

Before you decide if you need more education or training, you should first assess both your functional and work-content skills to see how they can be transferred to other jobs and occupations. Once you do this, you should be better prepared to communicate your qualifications to employers with a rich skills-based vocabulary.

Your Strengths

Regardless of what combination of work-content and functional skills you possess, a job search must begin with identifying your strengths. While you should be aware of your weaknesses, it's your strengths that will give your job search its needed direction. Without knowing your strengths, your job search will lack content and focus. After all, your goal should be to find a job that is fit for you rather than one you think you might be able to fit into. Of course, you also want to find a job for which there is a demand, as we noted in Chapter 5. This particular focus requires a well-defined approach to identifying and communicating your skills to others. You can best do this by asking the right questions about your strengths and then conducting a systematic self-assessment of what you do best – your skills and abilities.

Ask the Right Questions

Knowing the right questions to ask will save you time and steer you into productive job search channels from the very beginning. Asking the wrong questions can leave you frustrated. The questions must be understood from the perspectives of both employers and applicants.

Two of the most humbling questions you will encounter in your job search are *"Why should I hire you?"* and *"What are your weaknesses?"* While employers may not directly ask these questions, they are asking them nonetheless. If you can't answer these

> *Employers want to hire your value or strengths – not your weaknesses.*

questions in a positive manner – directly, indirectly, verbally, or non-verbally – your job search will likely founder and you will join the ranks of the unsuccessful and disillusioned job searchers who feel something is wrong with them. Individuals who have lost their jobs are particularly vulnerable to these questions since many have lowered self-esteem and self-image as a result of the job loss. Many such people focus on what is wrong rather than what is right about themselves. Such thinking creates self-fulfilling prophecies and is self-destructive in the job market. By all means avoid such negative thinking.

Employers want to hire your **value or strengths** – not your weaknesses. Since it is easier to identify and interpret weaknesses, employers look for indicators of your strengths by trying to identify your weaknesses. The more successful you are in communicating your strengths to employers, the better off you will be in relation to both employers and fellow applicants.

Strengths and Weaknesses

Unfortunately, many people work against their own best interests. Not knowing their strengths, they market their weaknesses by first identifying job vacancies and then trying to fit their "qualifications" into job descriptions. This approach often frustrates applicants; it presents a picture of a job market which is not interested in the applicant's strengths and it leads to the often-heard lament of frustrated job seekers – *"No one will hire me!"* This leads some people toward acquiring new skills which they hope will be marketable, even though they do not enjoy using them. Millions of individuals find themselves in such misplaced situations: the divorce lawyer who would rather be teaching in a university; the computer programmer who enjoys cooking and admires the cuisine of top chefs; the surgeon who is an accomplished pianist; or the salesman who is good at managing a community fund-raising drive. Your task is to avoid joining the ranks of the misplaced and unhappy workforce by first understanding your skills and then relating them to your values, interests, and goals. In so doing, you will be in a better position to target your job search toward jobs that should become especially rewarding and fulfilling.

Functional/Transferable Skills

We know most people stumble into jobs by accident. Some are in the right place at the right time to take advantage of opportunities. Others work hard at trying to fit into jobs posted on the Internet; listed in classified ads, employment agencies, and personnel offices; identified through friends and acquaintances; or found by knocking on doors. After 15 to 20 years in the work world, many people wish they had better planned their careers from the very start. All of a sudden they are unhappily locked into jobs because of retirement benefits and family responsibilities of raising children and meeting monthly mortgage payments.

After 10 to 20 years of work experience, most people have a good idea of what they don't like – not what they like to do.

After 10 or 20 years of work experience, most people have a good idea of what they don't like to do. While their values are more set than when they first began working, many people are still unclear as to what they do well and how their skills fit into the job market. What other jobs, for example, might they be qualified to perform? If they have the opportunity to change jobs or careers – either voluntarily or forced through termination – and find the time to plan the change, they can move into jobs and careers which fit their skills.

The key to understanding your non-technical strengths is to identify your transferable or functional skills. Once you have done this, you will be better prepared to identify what it is you want to do. Moreover, your self-image and self-esteem will improve. Better still, you will be prepared to communicate your strengths to others through a rich skills-based vocabulary. These outcomes are critically important for writing your resume and letters as well as for conducting informational and job interviews.

Let's illustrate the concept of functional/transferable skills for educators. Many educators view their skills in strict work-content terms – knowledge of a particular subject matter such as math, history, English, physics, or music. When looking for jobs outside education, many seek employment which will use their subject matter skills. But they soon discover non-educational institutions are not a ready market for such "skills."

On the other hand, educators possess many other skills that are directly transferable to business and industry. Unaware of these skills, many educators fail to communicate their strengths to others. For example, research shows that graduate students in the humanities most frequently possess these transferable skills, in order of importance:

1. critical thinking	7. general knowledge
2. research techniques	8. cultural perspective
3. perseverance	9. teaching ability
4. self-discipline	10. self-confidence
5. insight	11. imagination
6. writing	12. leadership ability

Most functional/transferable skills can be classified into two general skills and trait categories – organizational/interpersonal skills and personality/work-style traits:

Organizational and Interpersonal Skills

___ communicating	___ trouble-shooting
___ problem solving	___ implementing
___ analyzing/assessing	___ self-understanding
___ planning	___ understanding
___ decision-making	___ setting goals

__ innovating

__ thinking logically

__ evaluating

__ identifying problems

__ synthesizing

__ forecasting

__ tolerating ambiguity

__ motivating

__ leading

__ selling

__ performing

__ reviewing

__ attaining

__ team building

__ updating

__ coaching

__ supervising

__ estimating

__ negotiating

__ administering

__ conceptualizing

__ generalizing

__ managing time

__ creating

__ judging

__ controlling

__ organizing

__ persuading

__ encouraging

__ improving

__ designing

__ consulting

__ teaching

__ cultivating

__ advising

__ training

__ interpreting

__ achieving

__ reporting

__ managing

Personality and Work-Style Traits

__ diligent

__ patient

__ innovative

__ persistent

__ tactful

__ loyal

__ successful

__ versatile

__ enthusiastic

__ outgoing

__ expressive

__ adaptable

__ democratic

__ resourceful

__ determining

__ creative

__ open

__ objective

__ warm

__ honest

__ reliable

__ perceptive

__ assertive

__ sensitive

__ astute

__ risk taker

__ easygoing

__ calm

__ flexible

__ competent

__ punctual

__ receptive

__ diplomatic

__ self-confident

__ tenacious

__ discreet

__ talented

__ empathic

__ orderly	__ tidy
__ tolerant	__ candid
__ frank	__ adventuresome
__ cooperative	__ firm
__ dynamic	__ sincere
__ self-starter	__ initiator
__ precise	__ competent
__ sophisticated	__ diplomatic
__ effective	__ efficient

These are the types of skills you need to identify and then communicate to employers in your resumes and letters as well as during interviews.

Identify Your Skills

If you are just graduating from high school or college and do not know what you want to do, you probably should take a battery of vocational tests and psychological inventories to identify your values, interests, skills, aptitudes, and temperaments. We listed several such tests and inventories in Chapter 5. If you don't fall into these categories of job seekers, chances are you don't need complex testing. Indeed, you have experience, you have well defined values, and you know what you don't like in a job. Such testing may underwhelm when it identifies what you already know about yourself. Therefore, we outline several alternative skills identification exercises – simple to complex – assisting you at this stage. We recommend using the most complete and extensive activity – Motivated Skills Exercise (outlined in Chapter 8) – to gain a thorough understanding of your strengths.

> *These techniques stress your positives or strengths rather than identify your negatives or weaknesses.*

Use the following exercises to identify both your work-content and transferable skills. These self-assessment techniques stress your positives or strengths rather than identify your negatives or weaknesses. They should generate a rich vocabulary for communicating your "qualifications" to employers. Each exercise requires different investments of your time and effort as well as varying degrees of assistance from other people.

These exercises, however, should be used with caution. There is nothing magical nor particularly profound about them. Most are based upon a very simple and somewhat naive **deterministic theory of behavior** – your past patterns of behavior are good predictors of your future behavior. Not a bad theory for most individuals, but it is rather simplistic and disheartening for individuals who wish to, and can, break out of past patterns as they embark on a new future. Furthermore, most exercises are **historical devices**. They provide you with a clear picture of your past, which may or may not be particularly useful for charting your future. Nonetheless, these exercises do help individuals (1) organize data on themselves, (2) target their job search around clear objectives and skills, and (3) generate a rich vocabulary of skills and accomplishments for communicating strengths to potential employers.

If you feel these exercises are inadequate for your needs, by all means seek professional assistance from a testing or assessment center staffed by a licensed psychologist or certified career counselor. Many such centers can do in-depth testing which goes further than these self-directed skill exercises.

When using the following exercises, keep in mind that some individuals can and do change – often very dramatically – their behavior regardless of such deterministic and historical assessment devices. Much of the "motivation and success," "power of positive thinking," "thinking big," and "empowerment" literature identified in Chapter 2, for example, challenges the validity of these standardized assessment tests that are used to predict or pattern future individual behavior. So be careful how you use such information for charting your career future. You **can** change your future. But at least get to know yourself before making the changes.

Checklist Method

This is the simplest method for identifying your strengths. Review the different types of transferable skills outlined on pages 82-84. Place a "1" in front of the skills that **strongly** characterize you; assign a "2" to those skills that describe you to a **large extent**; put a "3" before those that describe you to **some extent**. When finished, review the lists and rank order the 10 characteristics that best describe you on each list.

The Skills Map

Richard Nelson Bolles has produced two well-known exercises for identifying transferable skills based upon John Holland's typology of work environments, which is the basis for the popular *Self-Directed Search®* *(SDS®)* and several other interest-oriented self-assessment inventories. Both are historical devices structured around a deterministic theory of behavior. In his book, **The Three Boxes of Life** (Ten Speed Press), he develops a checklist of 100 transferable skills. They are organized into 12 categories or types of skills: using hands, body, words, senses, numbers, intuition, analytical thinking, creativity, helpfulness, artistic abilities, leadership, and follow-through.

Bolles's second exercise, *"The Quick Job Hunting Map,"* expands upon this first one. The *"Map"* is a checklist of 222 skills. This exercise requires you to identify seven of your most satisfying accomplishments, achievements, jobs, or roles. After writing a page about each experience, you relate each to the checklist of 222 skills. The *"Map"* should give you a comprehensive picture of what skills you (1) use most frequently and (2) enjoy using in satisfying and successful settings. While this exercise may take six hours to complete, it yields an enormous amount of data on your past strengths. Furthermore, the *"Map"* generates a rich skills vocabulary for communicating your strengths to others. The *"Map"* is found in Bolles's **What Color Is Your Parachute?** and **What Color Is Your Parachute Workbook** (Ten Speed Press). These books can be ordered directly from Impact Publications by completing the order form at the end of this book.

Autobiography of Accomplishments

Write a lengthy essay about your life accomplishments. This could range from 20 to 100 pages. After completing the essay, go through it page by page to identify what you most enjoyed doing (working with different kinds of information, people, and things) and what skills you used most frequently as well as enjoyed using. Finally, identify those skills you wish to continue using. After analyzing and synthesizing this data, you should have a relatively clear picture of your strongest skills.

Computerized Assessment Programs

While the previous self-directed exercises required you to either respond to checklists of skills or reconstruct and analyze your past job experiences, several computerized self-assessment programs are designed to help individuals identify their skills. Many of the programs are available in career centers and some can be accessed online (inquire about Internet versions). Some of the most widely used programs, including two major programs we identified in Chapter 4, include:

- *Career Navigator*
- *Discover*
- *Guidance Information System* (GIS)
- *Self-Directed Search (SDS) Form R*
- *SIGI-Plus* (System of Interactive Guidance and Information)

Most of these comprehensive career planning programs do much more than just assess skills. As we will see in Chapter 8, they also integrate other key components in the career planning process – values, interests, goals, related jobs, college majors, education and training programs, and job search plans. These programs are widely available in schools, colleges, one-stop centers, and libraries across the country. You might check with the career or counseling center at a community college or your local one-stop center (visit www.service

> *Computerized assessment programs are widely available in schools, colleges, one-stop centers, and libraries across the country.*

locator.org and www.careeronestop.org for various locations) to see what computerized career assessment programs are available for your use. Relatively easy to use and taking one to two hours to complete, they generate a great deal of valuable career planning information. Many will print out a useful analysis of how your interests and skills are related to specific jobs and careers. Such programs come closest to our notion of a magic bullet – they generate a great deal of personal and professional data for such a small investment of time, effort, and money (you may be able to access these programs free of charge in your community).

Online Assessment

As we noted earlier, several companies now offer a variety of free and fee-based assessment tools via the Internet. Be sure to check out several of the assessment websites we outlined in Chapter 5 as well as check the websites related to the various self-assessment tests and inventories we summarized in Chapter 5. In general, fee-based assessment tools, such as *Myers-Briggs Type Indicator®*, *Strong Interest Inventory®*, and the *Self-Directed Search®*, will be your best choices. These are relatively sophisticated and reliable instruments available through licensing arrangements. They require certified professionals to administer the tools and interpret the results. Three websites in particular will give you online access to these major instruments:

- **SkillsOne**   www.skillsone.com
- **Self-Directed Search®**   www.self-directed-search.com
- **CareerLab**   www.careerlab.com

Be a smart shopper by acquiring the right resources to meet your needs.

The free online assessment tools are interesting to explore, but don't expect them to reveal a great deal of useful information for charting your career. In this business, you often get what you pay for. Don't be afraid to spend a little money (can be as little as $20 for the *Myers-Briggs Type Indicator®* taken through your local community college) to get what you need. But be a smart shopper by acquiring the right resources to meet your needs. In the long run, they will more than pay for themselves if they help you find the right job and career path.

7

Your Interests and Values

KNOWING WHAT YOU DO well – your skills, abilities, and aptitudes – is essential for understanding your strengths and for linking your capabilities to specific jobs that require those strengths. Usually referred to as one's "qualifications," your skills, abilities, and aptitudes also are important for targeting your job search and communicating your strengths to employers. However, just knowing your abilities and skills will not give your job search the direction it needs for finding a job that's right for you – one you both do well and enjoy doing. You also need to know your **work values and interests**. These are the basic building blocks for setting goals and targeting your abilities toward certain jobs and careers.

Take, for example, individuals who type 120 words a minute, design Web pages, or repair computers. While these people possess highly marketable skills, if they don't regularly enjoy using these skills and are more interested in working outdoors or with people, these abilities will not become **motivated skills**; these individuals will most likely not pursue jobs relating to word processing, the Internet, or computers, or they may be unhappy in jobs that use such skills. In the end, your interests and values will determine whether or not certain skills should play a central role in your job search.

Work, Leisure, and Home-Based Interests

We all have interests. Most change over time. Many of your interests may center on your present job whereas others relate to activities that define your hobbies and leisure activities. Other interests may relate to your dreams.

While many of the self-assessment tests and inventories identified in Chapter 4 focus on identifying and analyzing interests, the exercises included in this chapter are more open-ended and require self analysis rather than the involvement of a career professional. A good place to start identifying your interests is by examining the information and exercises found in both *The Guide to Occupational Exploration* and *The Enhanced Guide to Occupational Exploration*. Widely used by students and others first entering the job market, these are also relevant to individuals who already have work experience. These books classify all jobs in the United States into 12 interest areas. Examine the following list of interest areas. In the first column check those work areas that appeal to you. In the second column rank order those areas you checked in the first column. Start with "1" to indicate the most interesting:

Your Work Interests

Yes/No (x)	Ranking (1-12)	Interest Area
___	___	**Artistic:** An interest in creative expression of feelings or ideas.
___	___	**Scientific:** An interest in discovering, collecting, and analyzing information about the natural world, and in applying scientific research findings to problems in medicine, the life sciences, and the nature sciences.
___	___	**Plants and animals:** An interest in working with plants and animals, usually outdoors.

_____ _____ **Protective:** An interest in using authority to protect people and property.

_____ _____ **Mechanical:** An interest in applying mechanical principles to practical situations by using machines or hand tools.

_____ _____ **Industrial:** An interest in repetitive, concrete, organized activities done in a factory setting.

_____ _____ **Business detail:** An interest in organized, clearly defined activities requiring accuracy and attention to details (office settings).

_____ _____ **Selling:** An interest in bringing others to a particular point of view by personal persuasion, using sales and promotion techniques.

_____ _____ **Accommodating:** An interest in catering to the wishes and needs of others, usually on a one-to-one basis.

_____ _____ **Humanitarian:** An interest in helping others with their mental, spiritual, social, physical, or vocational needs.

_____ _____ **Leading and influencing:** An interest in leading and influencing others by using high-level verbal or numerical abilities.

_____ _____ **Physical performing:** An interest in physical activities performed before an audience.

The Guide to Occupational Exploration also includes other checklists relating to home-based and leisure activities that may or may not relate to your work interests. If you are unclear about your work interests, you might want to consult these other interest exercises. You may discover that some of your home-based and leisure activity interests should become your work interests. Examples of such interests include:

Leisure and Home-Based Interests

___ Acting in a play or amateur variety show.

___ Advising family members on their personal problems.

___ Announcing or emceeing a program.

___ Applying first aid in emergencies as a volunteer.

___ Building model airplanes, automobiles, or boats.

___ Building or repairing radio or television sets.

___ Buying large quantities of food or other products for an organization.

___ Campaigning for political candidates or issues.

___ Canning and preserving food.

___ Carving small wooden objects.

___ Coaching children or youth in sports activities.

___ Collecting experiments involving plants.

___ Conducting house-to-house or telephone surveys for a PTA or other organization.

___ Creating or styling hairdos for friends.

___ Designing your own greeting cards and writing original verses.

___ Developing film/printing pictures.

___ Doing impersonations.

___ Doing public speaking or debating.

___ Entertaining at parties or other events.

___ Helping conduct physical exercises for disabled people.

___ Making ceramic objects.

___ Modeling clothes for a fashion show.

___ Mounting and framing pictures.

___ Nursing sick pets.

___ Painting the interior or exterior of a home.

___ Playing a musical instrument.

___ Refinishing or re-upholstering furniture.

___ Repairing electrical household appliances.

___ Repairing the family car.

___ Repairing or assembling bicycles.

___ Repairing indoor plumbing.

___ Speaking on radio or television.

___ Taking photographs.

___ Teaching in Sunday School.

___ Tutoring pupils in school subjects.

___ Weaving rugs or making quilts.

___ Writing articles, stories, or plays.

___ Writing songs for club socials or amateur plays.

Indeed, many people turn hobbies or home activities into full-time jobs after deciding that such "work" is what they really enjoy doing.

Other popular exercises designed to identify your work interests include John Holland's *"The Self-Directed Search,"* which is found in his book, *Making Vocational Choices: A Theory of Careers*. It is also published as a separate testing instrument, *The Self-Directed Search – A Guide to Educational and Vocational Planning*. Developed from Holland's Vocational Preference Inventory, this popular self-administered, self-scored, and self-interpreted inventory helps individuals quickly identify what type of work environment they are motivated to seek – realistic, investigative, artistic, social, enterprising, or conventional – and aligns these work environments with lists of common occupational titles. An easy exercise to use, it gives you a quick overview of your orientation toward different types of work settings that interest you. Holland's self-directed search is also the basic framework used in developing Bolles's *"The Quick Job Hunting Map"* (see discussion on page 86).

For more sophisticated treatments of work interests, which are also validated through testing procedures, contact career counselors, women's centers, testing and assessment centers, or the appropriate publishers for information on these tests:

- *Career Assessment Inventory*
- *Career Exploration Inventory*
- *Jackson Vocational Interest Survey*
- *Kuder Occupational Interest Survey*
- *Leisure/Work Search Inventory*
- *Ohio Vocational Interest Survey*
- *Strong Interest Inventory®*
- *Vocational Interest Inventory*

Numerous other job and career interest inventories are also available. For further information, contact a career counselor or consult Educational Testing Service which compiles such tests. *The ETS Test Collection Catalog* (New York: Oryx Press) and *Tests* (Austin, TX: Pro-Ed), which are available in many library reference sections, lists most of these tests. The *Mental Measurements Yearbook* (Lincoln, NE: University of Nebraska Press) also surveys many of the major testing and assessment instruments.

Keep in mind that not all testing and assessment instruments used by career counselors are equally valid for career planning purposes. Indeed, many are over-used and of questionable validity. While the *Strong Interest Inventory®* appears to be the most relevant for career decision-making, the *Myers-Briggs Type Indicator®* has become an extremely popular instrument in recent years. It's used extensively by psychologists and career counselors for identifying 16 personality types. Widely used in pastoral counseling, student personnel, and business and religious organizations, it is more useful for classifying individual personality and decision-making styles than for identifying job fit and predicting career choices. For more information on this test, including online versions, contact: Consulting Psychologists Press, Inc. (Tel. 800-624-1765; websites: www.cpp.com and www.skillsone.com). Many career counselors who work with students in exploring careers find Holland's *The Self-Directed Search®* an excellent self-directed alternative to these professionally administered and interpreted tests. Our advice is to use several instruments, as well as our self-directed exercises, rather than rely on any one or two such devices. The more extensive tests, such as the Minnesota Importance Questionnaire (page 46), may prove most useful.

Key Work Values

Work values are those things you like to do. They give you pleasure and enjoyment. Most jobs involve a combination of likes and dislikes. By identifying what you both like and dislike about jobs, you should be able to better identify jobs that involve tasks that you will most enjoy.

Several exercises can help you identify your work values. First, identify what most satisfies you about work by completing the following exercise:

My Work Values

I prefer employment which enables me to:

____ contribute to society	____ be creative
____ have contact with people	____ supervise others
____ work alone	____ work with details
____ work with a team	____ gain recognition
____ compete with others	____ acquire security
____ make decisions	____ make money
____ work under pressure	____ help others
____ use power and authority	____ solve problems
____ acquire new knowledge	____ take risks
____ be a recognized expert	____ work at own pace

Select four work values from the above list which are the most important to you and list them in the space below. List any other work values (desired satisfactions) which were not listed above but are nonetheless important to you:

1. _____

2. _____

3. _____

4. _____

Another approach to identifying work values is outlined in *The Guide to Occupational Exploration*. If you feel you need to go beyond the above exercises, try this one. In the first column check those values that are most important to you. In the second column rank order the five most important values:

Ranking Work Values

Yes/No (x)	Ranking (1-5)	Work Values
____	____	**Adventure:** Working in a job that requires taking risks.
____	____	**Authority:** Working in a job in which you use your position to control others.
____	____	**Competition:** Working in a job in which you compete with others.
____	____	**Creativity and self-expression:** Working in a job in which you use your imagination to find new ways to do or say something.
____	____	**Flexible work schedule:** Working in a job in which you choose your hours to work.
____	____	**Helping others:** Working in a job in which you provide direct services to persons with problems.
____	____	**High salary:** Working in a job where many workers earn a large amount of money.
____	____	**Independence:** Working in a job in which you decide for yourself what work to do and how to do it.

_____ _____ **Influencing others:** Working in a job in which you influence the opinions of others or decisions of others.

_____ _____ **Intellectual stimulation:** Working in a job which requires a great amount of thought and reasoning.

_____ _____ **Leadership:** Working in a job in which you direct, manage, or supervise the activities of other people.

_____ _____ **Outside work:** Working out-of-doors.

_____ _____ **Persuading:** Working in a job in which you personally convince others to take certain actions.

_____ _____ **Physical work:** Working in a job which requires substantial physical activity.

_____ _____ **Prestige:** Working in a job which gives you status and respect in the community.

_____ _____ **Public attention:** Working in a job in which you attract immediate notice because of appearance or activity.

_____ _____ **Public contact:** Working in a job in which you daily deal with the public.

_____ _____ **Recognition:** Working in a job in which you gain public notice.

_____ _____ **Research work:** Working in a job in which you search for and discover new facts and develop ways to apply them.

_____ _____ **Routine work:** Working in a job in which you follow established procedures requiring little change.

—— —— **Seasonal work:** Working in a job in which you are employed only at certain times of the year.

—— —— **Travel:** Working in a job in which you take frequent trips.

—— —— **Variety:** Working in a job in which your duties change frequently.

—— —— **Work with children:** Working in a job in which you teach or care for children.

—— —— **Work with hands:** Working in a job in which you use your hands or hand tools.

—— —— **Work with machines or equipment:** Working in a job in which you use machines or equipment.

—— —— **Work with numbers:** Working in a job in which you use mathematics or statistics.

Second, develop a comprehensive list of your past and present **job frustrations and dissatisfactions**. This should help you identify negative factors you should avoid in future jobs.

My Job Frustrations and Dissatisfactions

List as well as rank order as many past and present things that frustrate or make you dissatisfied and unhappy in job situations:

Rank

1. _____ ____

2. _____ ____

3. _____ ____

4. _____ ____

5. _____ ____

6. _____ _____

7. _____ _____

8. _____ _____

9. _____ _____

10. _____ _____

Third, brainstorm a list of "Ten or More Things I Love to Do." Identify which ones could be incorporated into what kinds of work environments:

Ten or More Things I Love To Do

Item	Related Work Environment
1. _____	_____
2. _____	_____
3. _____	_____
4. _____	_____
5. _____	_____
6. _____	_____
7. _____	_____
8. _____	_____
9. _____	_____
10. _____	_____

Fourth, list at least 10 things you most enjoy about work and rank each item accordingly:

Ten Things I Enjoy the Most About Work

Rank

1. _____ _____

2. _____ _____

3. _____ _____

4. _____ _____

5. _____ _____

6. _____ _____

7. _____ _____

8. _____ _____

9. _____ _____

10. _____ _____

Fifth, you should also identify the types of interpersonal environments you prefer working in. Do this by specifying the types of people you like and dislike associating with:

Interpersonal Environments

Characteristics of people I like working with:	Characteristics of people I dislike working with:
_____	_____
_____	_____
_____	_____
_____	_____
_____	_____
_____	_____

_____   _____

_____   _____

Alternative Programs and Services

Several computerized self-assessment programs and online assessment services identified in Chapter 4 (pages 46-51) largely focus on career interests and values. Again, you may be able to get access to several of these programs through your local community college, one-stop career center, or library. Many of the testing and assessment websites identified on pages 53-54 include instruments for measuring interests and values.

As we stress throughout this book, no one test, instrument, or exercise will give you complete assessment information. Profit from redundancy by using a variety of approaches to answer your self-assessment questions in the process of identifying what you really want to do.

Project Your Values Into the Future

All of these exercises are designed to explore your past and present work-related values. At the same time, you need to project your values into the future. What, for example, do you want to do over the next 10 to 20 years? We'll return to this type of value question in Chapter 9 when we address the critical objective-setting stage of the career planning and job search process. Once you formulate your objective, you'll be prepared to take action that should lead to your dream job. Highly motivated and focused, you should be able to organize an effective job search that focuses laser-like on what you do well and enjoy doing.

8

Your Motivated Abilities and Skills (MAS)

ONCE YOU KNOW WHAT YOU really do well and enjoy doing, your next task should be to analyze those interests, values,
abilities, skills, and temperaments that form a **recurring motivated pattern**. This pattern is the single most important piece
of information you need to know about yourself in the whole self-
assessment process. Knowing your skills and abilities alone without
understanding how they relate to your interests, values, and temperament
will not give you the necessary direction for finding the job you want. You
simply **must** know your pattern. Once you do, your career planning and
job search activities may take on a whole new direction that will produce
amazing results. You'll be able to state a clear objective that will guide
you toward achieving your goals. So let's discover your pattern.

What's Your MAS?

The concept of motivated abilities and skills (MAS) enables us to relate
your interests and values to your skills and abilities. But how do we
identify your MAS beyond the questions and exercises outlined thus far?

Your pattern of motivated abilities and skills becomes evident once
you analyze your **achievements or accomplishments**. For it is your
achievements that tell us what you both do well and enjoy doing. If we

analyze and synthesize many of your achievements, we are likely to identify a **recurring pattern** that probably goes back to your childhood and which will continue to characterize your achievements in the future.

An equally useful exercise is to identify your **weaknesses** by analyzing your failures. These, too, would fall into recurring patterns. Understanding what your weaknesses are might help you avoid jobs and work situations that bring out the worst rather than the best in you. Indeed, you may learn more about yourself by analyzing your failures than by focusing solely on your accomplishments.

Another interesting approach is to examine how you have dealt with some of life's most **challenging situations**, such as an illness, accident, divorce, financial difficulties, starting a business, or a death in the family. Many of these difficult situations required character, drive, persistence, and problem-solving strategies beyond the ordinary. They may have drawn on inner strengths or a reservoir of skills you never knew you had but which occasionally came to the forefront when you were under extreme pressure. Moreover, your handling of these difficult situations might have led to life-altering consequences for you and those around you.

For now, let's focus on your positives rather than identify your negatives or how you coped with difficult situations. After you complete the strength exercises in this chapter, you may want to reverse the procedures to identify your weaknesses and challenges.

Numerous self-directed exercises can assist you in identifying your pattern of motivated abilities and skills. The basic requirements for making these exercises work for you are **time and analytical ability**. You must spend a great deal of time detailing your achievements by examining your history of accomplishments. Once you complete the historical reconstruction task, you must comb through your "stories" to identify recurring themes and patterns. This requires a high level of analytical ability which you may or may not possess. If analysis and synthesis are not two of your strong skills, you may want to seek assistance from a friend or professional who is good at analyzing and synthesizing information presented in narrative form. Career management firms such as BH Careers International (www.bhcareers.com) and People Management, Inc. (www.sima-pmi.com) are known for their use of this type of motivated pattern approach. Their versions of this assessment technique are presented in *Haldane's Best Resumes for Professionals* (Impact Publications) and **The Truth About You** (Ten Speed Press).

Several paper-and-pencil exercises are designed to help identify your pattern of motivated abilities and skills. We outline some of the most popular and thorough such exercises that have proved useful to thousands of people.

The Skills Map

Richard Nelson Bolles's *"Quick Job Hunting Map"* has become a standard self-assessment tool for thousands of job seekers and career changers who are willing to spend the time and effort necessary for discovering their pattern of motivated abilities and skills. Offering a checklist of over 200 skills organized around John Holland's concept of *"The Self-Directed Search"* for defining work environments (realistic, investigative, artistic, social, enterprising, and conventional), the *Map* requires you to identify seven of your most satisfying accomplishments, achievements, jobs, or roles. After describing each achievement, you analyze the details

> *Once you uncover your pattern, get prepared to acknowledge it and live with it in the future.*

of each in relation to the checklist of skills. Once you do this for all seven achievements, you should have a comprehensive picture of what skills you (1) use most frequently and (2) enjoy using in satisfying and successful settings. This exercise not only yields an enormous amount of information on your interests, values, skills, and abilities, it also assists you in the process of analyzing the data. If done properly, the *Map* should also generate a rich "skills" vocabulary which you should use in your resumes and letters as well as in interviews. For information on this *Map*, see page 86. The latest version of the *Map* can be found in Richard Nelson Bolles's **The What Color Is Your Parachute Workbook** (Ten Speed Press), which is available through Impact Publications by completing the order form at the end of this book or purchased online at www.impactpublications.com.

We highly recommend using the *Map* because of the ease in which it can be used. If you will spend the six to 20 hours necessary to complete it properly, the *Map* will give you some important information about yourself. Unfortunately, many people become overwhelmed by the exercise and either decide not to complete it, or they try to save time by not doing it according to the directions. You simply must follow the directions and spend the time and effort necessary if you want the maximum benefits from this very inexpensive exercise.

Keep in mind that, like most self-assessment devices, there is nothing magical about the *Map*. Its basic organizing principles are simple. Like other exercises designed to uncover your pattern of motivated abilities and skills, this one is based on a theory of historical determinism and probability. In other words, once you uncover your pattern, get prepared to acknowledge it and live with it in the future. There's a high probability that you will repeat your past patterns of behavior, especially if you focus on your achievements.

Autobiography of Accomplishments

Less structured than the *Map* device, this exercise requires you to write a lengthy essay about your life accomplishments. Your essay may run anywhere from 20 to 200 pages. After completing it, go through it page by page to identify what you most enjoyed doing (working with different kinds of data, people, processes, and objects) and what skills you used most frequently as well as enjoyed using. Finally, identify those skills you wish to continue using. After analyzing and synthesizing this data, you should have a relatively clear picture of your strongest skills.

This exercise requires a great deal of self-discipline and analytic skill (content analysis). To do it properly, you must write as much as possible, and in as much detail as possible, about your accomplishments. The richer the detail, the better will be your analysis. If you have difficulty analyzing your story, find someone who can assist you in distilling your accomplishments into a distinct set of behavioral patterns.

Motivated Skills Exercise

Our final exercise is one of the most complex and time-consuming self-assessment exercises. However, it yields some of the best data on motivated abilities and skills, and it is especially useful for those who feel they need a more thorough analysis of their past achievements. It's our preferred device which is used by many career counselors. Initially developed by Dr. Bernard Haldane, the father of modern career counseling, this exercise is variously referred to as *"Success Factor Analysis," "System to Identify Motivated Skills,"* or *"Intensive Skills Identification."*

This technique helps you identify which skills you **enjoy** using. While you can use this technique on your own, it is best to work with someone else. Since you will need six to eight hours to properly complete this exercise, divide your time into two or three work sessions.

The exercise consists of six steps. The steps follow the basic pattern of generating raw data, identifying patterns, analyzing the data through reduction techniques, and synthesizing the patterns into a transferable skills vocabulary. You need strong analytical skills to complete this exercise on your own. The six steps include:

1. **Identify 15-20 achievements:** While ideally you should inventory over 100-150 achievements, let's start by focusing on a minimum of 15-20 achievements. These consist of things you enjoyed doing, believe you did well, and felt a sense of satisfaction, pride, or accomplishment in doing. You can see yourself performing at your best and enjoying your experiences when you analyze your achievements. This information reveals your motivations since it deals entirely with your voluntary behavior. In addition, it identifies what is right with you by focusing on your positives and strengths. Identify achievements throughout your life, beginning with your childhood. Your achievements should relate to specific experiences – not general ones – and may be drawn from work, leisure, education, military, or home life. Put each achievement at the top of a separate sheet of paper on which you will further elaborate. For example, your achievements might appear as follows:

Sample Achievement Statements

"When I was 10 years old, I started a small paper route and built it up to the largest in my district."

"I started playing chess in ninth grade and earned the right to play first board on my high school chess team in my junior year."

"Learned to play the piano and often played for church services while in high school."

_____

"Designed, constructed, and displayed a dress for a 4-H demonstration project."

_____

"Played a major role in developing my high school website, which resulted in starting a small but very successful web design business at age 16 that helped finance my way through college."

_____

"Although I was small compared to other guys, I made the first string on my high school football team."

_____

"I graduated from high school with honors even though I was very active in school clubs and had to work part-time."

_____

"I was the first in my family to go to college and one of the few from my high school. Worked part-time and summers. A real struggle, but I made it."

_____

"Earned an 'A' grade on my senior psychology project from a real tough professor."

_____

"Finished my master's degree while working full-time and attending to important family responsibilities."

_____

"Proposed a chef's course for junior high boys. Got it approved. Developed it into a very popular elective."

_____

"Designed our house and had it constructed in time and under budget."

_____

"Taught myself advanced digital photo methods that resulted in winning first place in a prestigious photo contest of amateur photographers."

_____

"Organized a successful community effort that opposed developing a 10-acre historical site into a Wal-Mart shopping complex."

_____

"Raised two wonderful daughters who are studying to become medical doctors."

_____

2. Prioritize your seven most significant achievements.

Your Most Significant Achievements

1. _____
2. _____
3. _____
4. _____
5. _____
6. _____
7. _____

3. Write a full page on each of your prioritized achievements. You should describe:

- How you initially became involved.
- The details of **what you did** and **how you did it**.
- What was especially enjoyable or satisfying to you.

Use copies of the "Detailing Your Achievements" form on page 109 to outline your achievements.

Detailing Your Achievements

ACHIEVEMENT # ___: _____

_____

_____

1. How did I initially become involved? _____

   _____

   _____

   _____

2. What did I do? _____

   _____

   _____

   _____

   _____

3. How did I do it? _____

   _____

   _____

   _____

   _____

4. What was especially enjoyable about doing it?

   _____

   _____

   _____

   _____

4. **Elaborate on your achievements:** Have one or two other people interview you. For each achievement have them note on a separate sheet of paper any terms used to reveal your skills, abilities, and personal qualities. To elaborate details, the interviewer(s) may ask:

   - What was involved in the achievement?
   - What was your part?
   - What did you actually do?
   - How did you go about that?

   Clarify any vague areas by providing an example or illustration of what you actually did. Probe with the following questions:

   - Would you elaborate on one example of what you mean?
   - Could you give me an illustration?
   - What were you good at doing?

   This interview should clarify the details of your activities by asking only "what" and "how" questions. It should take 45 to 90 minutes to complete. Make copies of the "Strength Identification Interview" form on page 111 to guide you through this interview.

5. **Identify patterns by examining the interviewer's notes:** Together, identify the recurring skills, abilities, and personal qualities **demonstrated** in your achievements. Search for patterns. Your skills pattern should be clear at this point; you should feel comfortable with it. If you have questions, review the data. If you disagree with a conclusion, disregard it. The results must accurately and honestly reflect how you operate.

6. **Synthesize the information by clustering similar skills into categories:** For example, your skills might be grouped according to the cluster at the top of page 112.

Strength Identification Interview

Interviewee _____   Interviewer _____

INSTRUCTIONS: For each achievement experience, identify the **skills** and **abilities** the achiever actually demonstrated. Obtain details of the experience by asking *what* was involved with the achievement and *how* the individual made the achievement happen. Avoid "why" questions which tend to mislead. Ask for examples or illustrations of what and how.

Achievement #1:

Achievement #2:

Achievement #3:

Recurring abilities and skills:

Synthesized Skill Clusters

Investigate/Survey/Read	Teach/Train/Drill
Inquire/Probe/Question	Perform/Show/Demonstrate
Learn/Memorize/Practice	Construct/Assemble/Put together
Evaluate/Appraise/Assess	
Compare	Organize/Structure/Provide
	definition/Plan/Chart course
Influence/Involve/Get	Strategize/Coordinate
participation/Publicize	
Promote	Create/Design/Adapt/Modify

This exercise yields a relatively comprehensive inventory of your skills. The information will better enable you to use a **skills vocabulary** when identifying your objective, writing your resume and letters, and interviewing. If you are like many others who have successfully completed this exercise, your self-confidence and self-esteem should increase accordingly.

Other Alternatives

Several other techniques also can help you identify your motivated abilities and skills:

1. List all of your hobbies and analyze what you do in each, which ones you like the most, what skills you use, and your accomplishments.

2. Conduct a job analysis by writing about your past jobs and identifying which skills you used in each job. Cluster the skills into related categories and prioritize them according to your preferences.

3. Acquire a copy of Arthur F. Miller and Ralph T. Mattson's ***The Truth About You*** (now out of print) and work through the exercises found in the Appendix. While its overt religious message, extreme deterministic approach, and laborious exercises may turn off some users, you may find this book useful

nonetheless. This is an abbreviated version of the authors' SIMA (System for Identifying Motivated Abilities) technique used by their career counseling firm, People Management, Inc. (www.sima-pmi.com). If you need professional assistance, contact this firm directly. They can provide you with several alternative services consistent with the career planning philosophy and approach outlined in this chapter.

4. Complete John Holland's *"The Self-Directed Search (SDS®)."* You'll find it in his book, *Making Vocational Choices: A Theory of Vocational Personalities and Work Environments* or in a separate publication entitled *The Self-Directed Search – A Guide to Educational and Vocational Planning.* Also, check out the publisher's (Psychological Assessment Resources) website for an online version of the SDS®: www.self-directed-search. com.

Benefit From Redundancy

The self-directed MAS exercises generate similar information. They identify interests, values, abilities, and skills you already possess. While the many paper-and-pencil and computerized tests outlined in Chapter 4 (pages 45-52) may yield similar information, the self-directed exercises have three major advantages over the standardized tests: less expensive, self-monitored and evaluated, and measure motivation **and** ability.

Each exercise demands a different investment of time. Writing your life history and completing the Motivated Skills Exercise and Bolles's *Map* are the most time consuming. On the other hand, Holland's *"Self-Directed Search"* can be completed in a few minutes. But the more time you invest with each technique, the more useful information you will generate.

> *Employers rightfully believe that past performance is the best predictor of future performance. You need to clearly communicate your predictable "pattern of performance" to employers.*

We recommend creating redundancy by using at least two or three different techniques, such as the professionally administered *Myers-Briggs Type Indicator®* and *Strong Interest Inventory®*. This will help reinforce and confirm the validity of your observations and interpretations. If you have a great deal of work experience, we recommend using the more thorough exercises. The more you put into these techniques and exercises, the greater the benefit to other stages of your job search. You will be well prepared to target your job search toward specific jobs that fit your MAS as well as communicate your qualifications loudly and clearly to employers. A carefully planned career or career change should not do less than this.

Bridging Your Past and Future

Many people want to effortlessly know about their future. If you expect the self-assessment techniques in Chapters 6, 7, and 8 to spell out your future, you will be disappointed. Fortune tellers, horoscopes, positive thinking, spiritual advisors, and various forms of mysticism that look **outside** the individual may be what you need.

These are historical and deterministic devices that look **inside** the individual for answers to the future. They integrate past achievements, abilities, and motivations into a coherent framework for projecting future performance. They clarify past strengths and recurring motivations for targeting future jobs. Abilities and motivations are the **qualifications** employers expect for particular jobs. Qualifications consist of your past experience **and** your motivated abilities and skills.

The assessment techniques provide a bridge between your past and future. They treat your future preferences and performance as functions of your past experiences and demonstrated abilities. This common sense notion – **past performance is the best predictor of future performance** – is shared by employers, especially among those who increasingly conduct situational and behavior-based interviews that are designed to uncover such patterns.

Yet, employers hire a person's **future** rather than their past. And herein lies an important problem you can help employers overcome. Getting the job that is right for you entails communicating to prospective employers that you have the necessary qualifications. Indeed, employers will look for signs of your future productivity **for them**. Since you are an unknown and risky quantity for prospective employers, you must communicate evidence of your past productivity so they can better predict your future performance. This evidence is revealed clearly in your past achievements as outlined in our assessment techniques.

The overall value of using these assessment techniques is that they should enhance your occupational mobility over the long run. The major thrust of all these techniques is to identify abilities and skills which are **transferable** to different work environments. This is particularly important if you are making a career change. You must overcome employers' negative expectations and objections toward career changers by clearly communicating your transferable abilities and skills in the most positive terms possible. These assessment techniques are designed to do precisely that.

9

Your Objective

ONCE YOU HAVE IDENTIFIED YOUR motivated abilities and skills (MAS), you should be well prepared to develop a clear and purposeful objective for targeting your job search toward specific jobs, organizations, and employers. With a renewed sense of direction and versed in an appropriate language, you should be able to clearly communicate to prospective employers, using many interesting examples and stories of success, that you are a talented and purposeful individual who **achieves results**. Your objective must tell employers what you will **do for them** rather than what you want from them. It targets your pattern of accomplishments around employers' needs. In other words, your objective should be employer-centered rather than self-centered.

Mission Statements, Goals, and Objectives

Your objective is not the same as a mission statement, which is usually associated with the kind of person you would like to become. A mission statement is more closely associated with your purpose or significance in life and it might be identified through an obituary exercise – a statement of how you would like to be remembered after death.

Goals and objectives are statements of what you want to do in the future. When combined with an assessment of your interests, values, abilities, and skills, and related to specific jobs, they give your job search needed direction and meaning for the purpose of targeting specific employers. Without them, your job search may founder as you present an image of uncertainty and confusion to potential employers. Employers want to hire talented, enthusiastic, and purposeful individuals.

When you identify your strengths, you also create the necessary database and vocabulary for developing your job objective. Using this vocabulary, which is really the language of employers, you should be able to communicate your strengths to prospective employers.

Your objective should be employer- or work-centered rather than self-centered. It should reflect your honesty and integrity; it should not be "hyped."

If you fail to do the preliminary self-assessment work necessary for developing a clear objective, you will probably wander aimlessly in a highly decentralized, fragmented, and chaotic job market looking for interesting jobs you might fit into. Your goal, instead, should be to find a job or career that is compatible with your interests, motivations, skills, and talents as well as related to a vision of your future. In other words, try to find a job fit for you and your future rather than try to fit into a job that happens to be advertised and for which you think you can qualify. Remember, your ultimate goal should be to find a job and career you really love.

Your MAS and Vision of the Future

Depending on how you approach your job search, your goals can be largely a restatement of your past MAS patterns (Chapter 8) or a vision of your future. If you base your job search on an analysis of your motivated abilities and skills, you may prefer restating your past patterns as your present and future goals. On the other hand, you may want to establish a vision of your future and set goals that motivate you to achieve that vision through a process of self-transformation.

The type of goals you choose to establish will involve different processes. However, the strongest goals will be those that combine your motivated abilities and skills with a realistic vision of your future.

A Work- and Employer-Centered Focus

Your objective should be a concise statement of what you want to do and what you have to offer to an employer. The position you seek is "what you want to do"; your qualifications are "what you have to offer." Your objective should state your strongest qualifications for meeting employers' needs. It should communicate what you have to offer an employer without emphasizing what you expect the employer to do for you. In other words, your objective should be **work-centered**, not self-centered; it should not contain trite terms which emphasize what you want, such as give me a(n) "opportunity for advancement," "position working with people," "progressive company," or "creative position." Such terms are viewed as "canned" job search language which say little of value about you. Above all, your objective should reflect your honesty and integrity; it should not be "hyped."

> *The strongest goals will be those that combine your motivated abilities and skills with a realistic vision of your future.*

Identifying what it is you want to do can be one of the most difficult job search tasks. Indeed, most job hunters lack clear objectives. Many engage in a random and somewhat mindless search for jobs by identifying available job opportunities and then adjusting their skills and objectives to fit specific job openings. While you can get a job using this approach, you may be misplaced and unhappy with what you find. You will fit into a job rather than find a job that is fit for you.

Knowing what you want to do can have numerous benefits. First, you define the job market rather than let it define you. The inherent fragmentation and chaos of the job market should be advantageous for you, because it enables you to systematically organize job opportunities around your specific objectives and skills. Second, you will communicate professionalism to prospective employers. They will receive a precise indication of your interests, qualifications, and purposes, which places you ahead of most other applicants. Third, being purposeful means being able to com-municate to employers what you really want to do. Employers are not interested in hiring indecisive and confused individuals who will probably have difficulty taking initiative because they really don't know what they should be doing in the first place. Employers want to know what it is you can and will do **for them**. With a clear objective – based upon a thorough understanding of your motivated skills and interests – you can take control of the situation as you demonstrate your value to employers.

Finally, few employers really know what they want in a candidate. Like most job seekers, employers often lack clear employment objectives and knowledge about how the job market operates. If you know what you want and can help the employer define his or her "needs" as your objective, you will have achieved a tremendously advantageous position in the job market.

A Realistic Objective

Your objective should communicate that you are a **purposeful individual who achieves results**. It can be stated over different time periods as well as at various levels of abstraction and specificity. You can identify short, intermediate, and long-range objectives and very general to very specific objectives. Whatever the case, it is best to know your prospective audience before deciding on the type of objective. Your objective should reflect your career interests as well as employers' needs.

Objectives also should be **realistic**. You may want to become president of the United States or solve all the world's problems. However, these objectives are probably unrealistic. While they may represent your ideals and fantasies, you need to be more realistic in terms of what you can personally accomplish in the immediate future given your particular skills, pattern of accomplishments, level of experience, and familiarity with the job market. What, for example, are you prepared to deliver to prospective employers over the next few months? While it is good to set challenging objectives, you can overdo it. Refine your objective by thinking about the next major step or two you would like to make in your career advance-ment. Develop a realistic action plan that focuses on the details of progressing your career one step at a time. By all means avoid making a grandiose leap outside reality!

Incorporate Your Dreams

Even after identifying your abilities and skills, specifying an **objective** can be the most difficult and tedious step in the job search process; it can stall the resume writing process indefinitely. This simple one-sentence, 25-word statement can take days or weeks to formulate and clearly define. Yet, it must be specified prior to writing the resume and engaging in other job search steps. An objective gives meaning and direction to all other activities.

Your objective should be viewed as a function of several influences. Since you want to build upon your strengths and you want to be realistic, your abilities and skills will play a central role in formulating your work objective. At the same time, you do not want your objective to become a function solely of your past accomplishments and skills. You may be very skilled in certain areas, but you may not want to use these skills in the future. As a result, your values and interests filter which skills you will or will not incorporate into your work objective.

Overcoming the problem of historical determinism – your future merely reflecting your past – requires incorporating additional components into defining your objective. One of the most important is your ideals, fantasies, or dreams. Everyone engages in these, and sometimes they come true. Your ideals, fantasies, or dreams may include making $1,000,000 by age 40; owning a Mercedes-Benz and a Porsche; taking trips to Rio, Hong Kong, and Rome; owning your own business; developing financial independence; writing a best-selling novel; solving major social problems; or winning the Nobel Peace Prize. If your fantasies require more money than you are now making, you will need to incorporate monetary considerations into your work objective. For example, if you have these fantasies, but your sense of realism tells you that your objective is to move from a $40,000 a year position to a $42,000 a year position, you will be going nowhere – unless you can fast-track in your new position. Therefore, you will need to set a higher objective to satisfy your fantasies.

You can develop realistic objectives many different ways. We don't claim to have a new or magical formula, only one which has worked for many individuals. We assume you are capable of making intelligent career decisions if given sufficient data. Using redundancy once again, our approach is designed to provide you with sufficient corroborating data from several sources and perspectives so that you can make preliminary decisions. If you follow our steps in setting a realistic objective, you should be able to give your job search clear direction.

Four major steps are involved in developing a work objective. Each step can be implemented in a variety of ways:

STEP 1: Develop or obtain basic data on your functional/transferable skills, which we discussed in Chapter 6.

STEP 2: Acquire corroborating data about yourself from other people, tests, and yourself. Several resources are available for this purpose:

A. **From other people:** Ask three to five individuals whom you know well to evaluate you according to the questions in the "Strength Evaluation" form on page 122. Explain to them that you believe their candid appraisal will help you gain a better understanding of your strengths and weaknesses from the perspectives of others. Make copies of this form and ask your evaluators to complete and return it to a designated third party who will share the information – but not the respondent's name – with you.

B. **From vocational tests:** Although we prefer self-generated data, vocationally oriented tests can help clarify, confirm, and translate your understanding of yourself into occupational directions. If you decide to use vocational tests, contact a professional career counselor who can administer and interpret the tests. We suggest several of the following tests:

- *Myers-Briggs Type Indicator®*
- *Strong Interest Inventory®*
- *Self-Directed Search (SDS)®*
- *Campbell Interest and Skill Survey*
- *Keirsey Character Sorter*
- *Birkman Method*
- *Enneagram*
- *FIRO-B®*

Strength Evaluation

TO: _____

FROM: _____

I am going through a career assessment process and thought you would be an appropriate person to ask for assistance. Would you please candidly respond to the questions below? Your comments will be given to me by the individual designed below; s/he will not reveal your name. Your comments will be used for advising purposes only. Thank you.

What are my strengths?

What weak areas might I need to improve?

In your opinion, what do I need in a job or career to make me satisfied?

Please return to: _____

- *California Psychological Inventory (CPI)*
- *16 Personality Factors Profile*
- *Edwards Personal Preference Schedule*
- *Kuder Occupational Interest Survey*
- *APTICOM*
- *Jackson Vocational Interest Survey*
- *Vocational Interest Inventory*
- *Career Assessment Inventory*
- *Temperament and Values Inventory*

C. From yourself: Numerous alternatives are available for you to practice redundancy. Refer to the exercises in Chapter 7 that assist you in identifying your work values, job frustrations and dissatisfactions, things you love to do, things you enjoy most about work, and your preferred interpersonal environments.

STEP 3: Project your values and preferences into the future by completing simulation and creative thinking exercises:

A. Ten Million Dollar Exercise: First, assume that you are given a $10,000,000 gift; now you don't have to work. Since the gift is restricted to your use only, you cannot give any part of it away. What will you do with your time? At first? Later on? Second, assume that you are given another $10,000,000, but this time you are required to give it all away. What kinds of causes, organizations, charities, etc. would you support? Complete the following form in which you answer these questions:

What Will I Do With Two $10,000,000 Gifts?

First gift is restricted to my use only:

_____

_____

_____

Second gift must be given away:

_____

_____

_____

B. Obituary Exercise: Make a list of the most important things you would like to do or accomplish before you die. Two alternatives are available for doing this. First, make a list in response to this lead-in statement: *"Before I die, I want to..."*

Before I Die, I Want to . . .

1. _____

_____

2. _____

_____

3. _____

_____

4. _____

_____

5. _____

_____

6. _____

_____

7. _____

_____

8. _____

_____

9. _____

_____

10. _____

_____

Second, write a newspaper article which is actually your obituary for 10 years from now. Stress your accomplishments over the coming 10-year period.

My Obituary

Obituary for Mr./Ms. _____ to appear in the _____ Newspaper in 20____.

_____

_____

_____

_____

_____

_____

_____

_____

_____

_____

_____

_____

_____

_____

_____

_____

C. **My Ideal Work Week:** Starting with Monday, place each day of the week as the headings on seven sheets of paper. Develop a daily calendar with 30-minute intervals, beginning at 7am and ending at midnight. Your calendar should consist of a 118-hour week. Next, beginning at 7am on Monday (sheet one), identify the **ideal activities** you would enjoy doing, or need to do, for each 30-minute segment during the day. Assume you are capable of doing anything; you have no constraints except those you impose on yourself. Furthermore, assume that your work schedule consists of 40 hours per week. How will you fill your time? Be specific.

My Ideal Work Week

Monday

am	pm
7:00 _____	4:00 _____
7:30 _____	4:30 _____
8:00 _____	5:00 _____
8:30 _____	5:30 _____
9:00 _____	6:00 _____
9:30 _____	6:30 _____
10:00 _____	7:00 _____
10:30 _____	7:30 _____
11:00 _____	8:00 _____
11:30 _____	8:30 _____
Noon _____	9:00 _____
12:30 _____	9:30 _____
pm	10:00 _____
1:00 _____	10:30 _____
1:30 _____	11:00 _____
2:00 _____	11:30 _____

2:30 _____	12:00 _____
3:00 _____	Continue for Tuesday,
	Wednesday, Thursday,
3:30 _____	and Friday

D. **My Ideal Job Description:** Develop your ideal future job. Be sure you include:

- Specific interests you want to build into your job
- Work responsibilities
- Working conditions
- Earnings and benefits
- Interpersonal environment
- Working circumstances, opportunities, and goals

Description of My Ideal Job

_____

_____

_____

_____

_____

_____

_____

_____

_____

_____

_____

_____

_____

_____

_____

_____

_____

_____

Use "My Ideal Job Specifications" on page 129 to outline your ideal job. After completing this exercise, synthesize the job and write a detailed paragraph which describes the kind of job you would most enjoy.

STEP 4: Test your objective against reality. Evaluate and refine it by conducting market research, a force field analysis, library research, and informational interviews.

A.   Market Research: Four steps are involved in conducting this research:

> **1. Products or services:** Based upon all other assessment activities, make a list of what you **do** or **make**:

Products/Services I Do or Make

1. _____

2. _____

3. _____

4. _____

5. _____

6. _____

7. _____

8. _____

9. _____

10. _____

My Ideal Job Specifications

Job Interests	Work Responsibilities	Working Conditions	Earnings /Benefits	Circumstances / Opportunities / Goals

2. **Market:** Identify who needs, wants, or buys what you do or make. Be very specific. Include individuals, groups, and organizations. Then, identify **what** specific **needs** your products or services fill. Next, assess the **results** you achieve with your products or services.

The Market for My Products/Services

Individuals, groups, and organizations needing me:

1. _____
2. _____
3. _____
4. _____
5. _____

Needs I fulfill:

1. _____
2. _____
3. _____
4. _____
5. _____

Results/outcomes/impacts of my products/services:

1. _____
2. _____
3. _____
4. _____
5. _____

3. **New Markets:** Brainstorm a list of **who else** needs your products or services. Think about ways of expanding your market. Next, list any new needs your current or new market has which you might be able to fill:

Developing New Needs

Who else needs my products/services?

1. _____
2. _____
3. _____
4. _____
5. _____

New ways to expand my market:

1. _____
2. _____
3. _____
4. _____
5. _____

New needs I should fulfill:

1. _____
2. _____
3. _____
4. _____
5. _____

4. **New products and/or services:** List any new products or services you can offer and any new needs you can satisfy:

New Products/Services I Can Offer

1. _____
2. _____
3. _____
4. _____
5. _____

New Needs I Can Meet

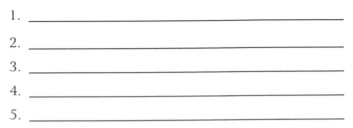

1. _____

2. _____

3. _____

4. _____

5. _____

B. **Force Field Analysis:** Once you develop a tentative or firm objective, force field analysis can help you understand the various internal and external forces affecting the achievement of your objective. Force field analysis follows this sequence of activities:

■ **Clearly state your objective or course of action.** Make sure it's based upon your MAS and is employer-oriented rather than self-centered.

■ **List the positive and negative forces affecting your objective.** Specify the internal and external forces working **for** and **against** you in terms of who, what, where, when, and how much. Estimate the impact of each on your objective.

■ **Analyze the forces.** Assess the importance of each force upon your objective and its probable effect upon you. Some forces may be irrelevant to your goal. You may need additional information to make a thorough analysis.

■ **Maximize positive forces and minimize negative ones.** Identify actions you can take to strengthen positive forces and to neutralize, overcome, or reverse negative forces. Focus on real, important, and probable key forces.

■ **Assess the feasibility of attaining your objective** and, if necessary, modifying it in light of new information.

C. **Conduct Online and Library Research:** This research should strengthen and clarify your objective. Consult various reference materials on alternative jobs and careers. Most of these resources are available in print form at your local library or bookstore. Some are available in electronic versions online. If you explore the numerous company profiles and career sites available on the Internet, you should be able to tap into a wealth of information on alternative jobs and careers. Two good resources for initiating online research are Margaret Riley Dikel's *The Guide to Internet Job Search* (McGraw-Hill) and Pam Dixon's *Job Searching Online for Dummies* (IDG Books). For directories to key employment websites, see Ron and Caryl Krannich, *America's Top Internet Job Sites* and *The Directory of Websites for International Jobs* (Impact Publications); Bernard Haldane Associates, *Haldane's Best Employment Websites for Professionals* (Impact Publications); and Gerry Crispin and Mark Mehler, *CareerXroads* (MMC Group). Many of the resources traditionally found in libraries are available online. The following websites function as excellent gateway sites, online databases, and research tools:

- CEO Express   www.ceoexpress.com
- Hoover's Online   www.hoovers.com
- Dun and Bradstreet's
  Million Dollar Databases   www.dnbmdd.com/mddi
- Corporate Information   www.corporateinformation. com
- BizTech Network   www.brint.com
- AllBusiness   www.allbusiness.com
- BizWeb   www.bizweb.com
- Business.com   www.business.com
- America's CareerInfoNet   www.acinet.org
- Newspapers USA   www.newspapers.com
- Salary.com   www.salary.com
- Annual Report Service   www.annualreportservice.com
- Bloomberg   www.bloomberg.com
- Chamber of Commerce   www.chamberofcommerce. com

- CNN Money   http//money.cnn.com
- Daily Stocks   www.dailystocks.com
- The Corporate Library www.thecorporatelibrary.com
- Forbes Lists   www.forbes.com/lists
- Fortune 500   www.fortune.com
- Harris InfoSource   www.harrisinfo.com
- Inc. 500   www.inc.com/500
- Moodys   www.moodys.com
- Motley Fool   www.fool.com
- NASDAQ   www.nasdaq.com
- One Source Corp Tech   www.onesource.com
- Standard & Poors   www.standardandpoors.com
- The Street   www.thestreet.com
- Thomas Regional   www.thomasregional.com
- Thomas Register   www.thomasregister.com

Career and Job Alternatives

- *25 Jobs That Have It All*
- *50 Cutting Edge Jobs*
- *Almanac of American Employers*
- *Almanac of American Employers Mid-Size Firms*
- *America's Top 100 Jobs for People Without a Four-Year Degree*
- *Enhanced Guide for Occupational Exploration*
- *Guide to Occupational Exploration*
- *Quick Prep Careers*
- *Occupational Outlook Handbook*
- *Occupational Outlook Quarterly*
- *O*NET Dictionary of Occupational Titles*

Industrial Directories

- *Dun and Bradstreet's Middle Market Directory*
- *Dun and Bradstreet's Million Dollar Directory*
- *Encyclopedia of Business Information Sources*
- *Geography Index*
- *Poor's Register of Corporations, Directors, and Executives*

- *Standard Directory of Advertisers*
- *The Standard Periodical Directory*
- *Standard and Poor's Industrial Index*
- *Standard Rate & Data Business Publications Directory*
- *Thomas' Register of American Manufacturers*

Associations

- *Associations USA*
- *Encyclopedia of Associations*
- *National Trade and Professional Associations*
- Access thousands of associations online through: www.ipl.org/ref/AON and www.asaenet.org.

Government Sources

- *The Book of the States*
- *Congressional Directory*
- *Congressional Staff Directory*
- *Congressional Yellow Book*
- *Federal Directory*
- *Federal Yellow Book*
- *Municipal Yearbook*
- *Taylor's Encyclopedia of Government Officials*
- *United Nations Yearbook*
- *United States Government Manual*
- *Washington Information Directory*

Newspapers

- Major city newspapers and trade newspapers. Many are available online through these gateway sites: www.ipl.org/reading/news, http://.newsdirectory.com, www.newspaperlinks.com, and www.newspapers.com.
- Your targeted city newspaper – the Sunday edition.

Business Publications

- *Business 2.0, Business Week, Economist, Fast Company, Inc., Forbes, Fortune, Harvard Business Review, Newsweek, Smart Money, Time, U.S. News and World Report, Wired.* Many of these and other business-oriented publications can be viewed online through this terrific website: www.CEO Express.com.

- Annual issues of publications surveying the best jobs and employers for the year: *Money, Fortune, Forbes,* and *U.S. News and World Report.* Several of these reports and publications are available online: www.money.com, www. fortune.com, and www.forbes.com/lists.

Other Library Resources

- Trade journals
- Publications of Chambers of Commerce; state manufacturing associations; and federal, state, and local government agencies
- Telephone books – The Yellow Pages
- Books on "how to get a job" (see order form at the end of this book and www.impactpublications.com)

D. **Conduct Informational Interviews:** This may be the most useful way to clarify and refine your objective.

After completing these steps, you will have identified what it is you **can** do (abilities and skills), enlarged your thinking to include what it is you would **like** to do (aspirations), and probed the realities of implementing your objective. Thus, setting a realistic work objective is a function of the diverse considerations outlined on page 137.

Your work objective is a function of both subjective and objective information as well as combines idealism with realism. We believe the strongest emphasis should be placed on your competencies and should include a broad database. Your work objective is realistic in that it is tempered by your past experiences, accomplishments, skills, and current

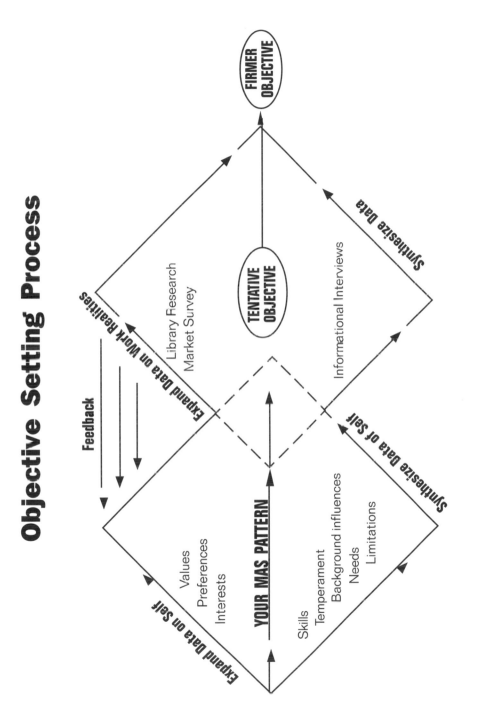

Objective Setting Process

FIRMER OBJECTIVE

TENTATIVE OBJECTIVE

Synthesize Data

Library Research
Market Survey

Informational Interviews

Expand Data on Work Realities

Feedback

Synthesize Data of Self

Values
Preferences
Interests

YOUR MAS PATTERN

Skills
Temperament
Background influences
Needs
Limitations

Expand Data on Self

research. An objective formulated in this manner permits you to think beyond your past experiences.

State a Functional Objective

Your job objective should be oriented toward skills and results or outcomes. You can begin by stating a functional job objective at two different levels: a general objective and a specific one for communicating your qualifications to employers both on resumes and in interviews. Thus, this objective-setting process sets the stage for other key job search activities. For the general objective, begin with the statement:

Stating Your General Objective

I would like a job where I can use my ability to _____, which will result in _____.

The objective in this statement is both a **skill** and an **outcome**. For example, you might state:

Skills-Based and Results-Oriented Objective

I would like a job where my experience in program development, supported by innovative decision-making and systems engineering abilities, will result in an expanded clientele and a more profitable organization.

At a second level you may wish to re-write this objective in order to target it at various consulting firms. For example, on your resume it becomes:

Job-Targeted Objective

An increasingly responsible research position in consulting, where proven decision-making and systems engineering abilities will be used for improving organizational productivity.

The following are examples of weak and strong objective statements. Various styles are also presented.

Weak Objectives

Management position which will use business administration degree and will provide opportunities for rapid advancement.

A position in social services which will allow me to work with people in a helping capacity.

A position in Human Resources with a progressive firm.

Sales Representative with opportunity for advancement.

Stronger Objectives

*To use computer science training in **software development** for designing and implementing operating systems.*

A public relations position which will maximize opportunities to develop and implement programs, to organize people and events, and to communicate positive ideas and images. Effective in public speaking and in managing a publicity/promotional campaign.

A position as a General Sales Representative with a pharmaceutical house which will use chemistry background and ability to work on a self-directed basis in managing a marketing territory.

A position in data analysis where skills in mathematics, computer programming, and deductive reasoning will contribute to new systems development.

Retail Management position which will use sales/customer service experience and creative abilities for product display and merchandising. Long term goal: Progression to merchandise manager with corporate-wide responsibilities for product line.

Responsible position in investment research and analysis. Interests and skills include securities analysis, financial planning, and portfolio management. Long range goal: to become a Chartered Financial Analyst.

It is important to relate your objective to your audience. While you definitely want a good job that pays well, your audience wants to know what you can do for them in exchange for a good paying job. Remember, your objective should be work-centered, not self-centered.

> *Your objective will become the key to organizing all other elements in your job search.*

Your objective will become the key to organizing all other elements in your job search. It should become the central organizing element on your resume. It gives meaning and direction to your job search. Your objective says something very important about how you want to conduct your life with the employer. It gives them an important indicator of the value you will bring to this job. Most important of all, it tells them who you really are in terms of your key values and accomplishments – a short answer to the big question of *"Why should I hire you?"*

10

Putting It All Together

NOW THAT YOU HAVE a clear idea of what you want to do, it's time to put this foundational information together into a well organized and effective job search. Elsewhere *(The Job Hunting Guide* and *Change Your Job, Change Your Life)* we examine the whole job search process in detail. In this chapter we present an abbreviated version in graphic, test, and evaluation forms to get you started in the right direction. These visuals and instruments examine your knowledge, skills, attitudes, and behavior for conducting a successful job search.

Our purpose here is to outline the basic elements that go into organizing a well targeted job search as well as share an effective strategy for implementing your best laid plans. For in the end, all the great testing and planning will be for naught if you fail to put together an action plan for implementing your job search.

Organizing an Effective Job Search

The figure on page 142 portrays the relationship among elements in a successful job search. From self-assessment to negotiating salary, the job search consists of a seven-step process. Since the individual job search steps are interrelated, they should be followed in the suggested sequence.

Job Search Steps and Stages

7. Negotiate salary and terms of employment

6. Manage Job Interviews

5. Conduct informational/ networking interviews

4. Produce resumes and job search letters

3. Research individuals, organizations, communities, and jobs

2. Specify a job/career objective

1. Identify motivated skills and abilities

As we've noted throughout this book, if you fail to properly complete the initial self-assessment steps (Steps 1 and 2), your job search may become haphazard, aimless, and costly. For example, you should never write a resume (Step 3) before first conducting an assessment of your skills (Step 1) and identifying your objective (Step 2). Relating Step 1 to Step 2 is especially critical to the successful implementation of all other job search steps. You **must** complete Steps 1 and 2 **before** continuing on to the other steps. Steps 3 to 6 may be conducted simultaneously because they complement and reinforce one another.

Try to sequence your job search as closely to these steps as possible. The true value of this sequencing will become very apparent as you implement your plan.

Plan to Take Action

While we recommend that you plan your job search, we also caution you to avoid the excesses of too much planning. Planning should not be all-consuming. It makes sense because it focuses attention and directs action toward specific targets. It requires you to set goals and develop strategies for achieving the goals. However, too much planning can blind you to unexpected occurrences and opportunities – that wonderful experience called serendipity. Given the highly decentralized and chaotic nature of the job market, you want to do just enough planning so you will be in a position to take advantage of what will inevitably be unexpected occurrences and opportunities arising from your planned job search activities. Therefore, as you plan your job search, be sure you are flexible enough to take advantage of new opportunities.

Based on our sequence of job search steps on page 142, we outline on page 144 a hypothetical plan for conducting an effective job search. This plan incorporates the individual job search activities over a six-month period. If you phase in the first five job search steps during the initial three to four weeks and continue the final four steps in subsequent weeks and months, you should begin receiving job offers within two to three months after initiating your job search. Interviews and job offers can come anytime – often unexpectedly – as you conduct your job search. An average time is three months, but it can occur within a week or take as long as five months or more. If you plan, prepare, and persist at the job search, the pay-off will be job interviews and offers.

Organization of Job Search Activities

Activity	Weeks																							
	1	2	3	4	5	6	7	8	9	10	11	12	13	14	15	16	17	18	19	20	21	22	23	24
▪ Thinking, questioning, listening, evaluating, adjusting				▓																				
▪ Identifying abilities and skills	▓																							
▪ Setting objectives			▓																					
▪ Writing resume					▓																			
▪ Conducting research				▓																				
▪ Prospecting, referrals, networking				▓																				
▪ Interviewing										▓		▓		▓		▓						▓		
▪ Receiving and negotiating job offers										▓		▓				▓		▓				▓		▓

While three months may seem a long time, especially if you have just lost your job and you need work immediately, you can shorten your job search time by increasing the frequency of your individual job search activities. If you are job hunting on a full-time basis, you may be able to cut your job search time in half. But don't expect to get a job – especially a job that's right for you – within a week or two. Job hunting requires time and hard work – perhaps the hardest work you will ever do – but if done properly, it pays off with a job that is right for you.

20 Principles for Job Search Success

Success is determined by more than just a good plan being implemented. We know success is not determined primarily by intelligence, time management, or luck. Based upon experience, theory, research, common sense, and acceptance of some self-transformation principles, we believe you will achieve job search success by following most of these 20 principles:

1. **You should work hard at finding a job:** Make this a daily endeavor and involve your family. Focus on specifics.

2. **You should not be discouraged by setbacks:** You are playing the odds, so expect disappointments and handle them in stride. You will get many "no's" before finding the one "yes" which is right for you.

3. **You should be patient and persevere:** Expect three to six months of hard work before you connect with the job that's right for you.

4. **You should be honest with yourself and others:** Honesty is always the best policy. But don't be naive and stupid by confessing your negatives and shortcomings to others.

5. **You should develop a positive attitude toward yourself:** Nobody wants to employ guilt-ridden people with inferiority complexes. Focus on your positive characteristics.

6. **You should associate with positive and successful people:** Finding a job largely depends on how well you relate to others. Avoid associating with negative and depressing people who complain and have a "you-can't-do-it" attitude. Run with winners who have a positive "can-do" outlook on life.

7. **You should set goals:** You should have a clear idea of what you want and where you are going. Without these, you will present a confusing and indecisive image to others. Clear goals direct your job search into productive channels. Setting high goals will help make you work hard in getting what you want.

8. **You should plan:** Convert your goals into action steps that are organized as short, intermediate, and long-range plans.

9. **You should get organized:** Translate your plans into activities, targets, names, addresses, telephone numbers, and materials. Develop an efficient and effective filing system and use a large calendar to set time targets, record appointments, and compile useful information.

10. **You should be a good communicator:** Take stock of your oral, written, and nonverbal communication skills. How well do you communicate? Since most aspects of your job search involve communicating with others, and communication skills are one of the most sought-after skills, always present yourself well both verbally and nonverbally.

11. **You should be energetic and enthusiastic:** Employers are attracted to positive people. They don't like negative and depressing people who toil at their work. Generate enthusiasm both verbally and nonverbally. Check on your telephone voice – it may be more unenthusiastic than your face-to-face voice.

12. **You should ask questions:** Your best information comes from asking questions. Learn to develop intelligent questions that are non-aggressive, polite, and interesting to others. But don't ask too many questions and thereby become a bore.

13. **You should be a good listener:** Being a good listener is often more important than being a good questioner or talker. Learn to improve your face-to-face listening behavior (nonverbal cues) as well as remember and use information gained from others. Make others feel they enjoyed talking with you, i.e., you are one of the few people who actually **listens** to what they say.

14. **You should be civil, which means being polite, courteous, and thoughtful:** Treat gatekeepers, especially receptionists, like human beings. Avoid being aggressive. Try to be polite, courteous, and thoughtful. Your social graces are being observed. Remember to send thank you letters – a very thoughtful thing to do in a job search. Even if rejected, thank employers for the "opportunity." They may later have additional opportunities, and they will be more likely to remember you.

15. **You should be tactful:** Watch what you say to others about other people. Don't be a gossip, back-stabber, or confessor.

16. **You should maintain a professional stance:** Be neat in what you do and wear, and speak with the confidence, authority, and maturity of a professional.

17. **You should demonstrate your intelligence and competence:** Present yourself as someone who gets things done and achieves results – a **producer**. Employers generally seek people who are bright, hard working, responsible, communicate well, have positive personalities, maintain good interpersonal relations, are likable, observe dress and social codes, take initiative, are talented, possess expertise in particular areas, use good judgment, are cooperative, trustworthy, and loyal, generate confidence and credibility, and are conventional. In other words, they like people who score in the "excellent" to "outstanding" categories of a performance evaluation.

18. **You should not overdo your job search:** Don't engage in overkill and bore everyone with your "job search" stories. Achieve balance in everything you do. Occasionally take a few days off to do nothing related to your job search. Develop a system of

incentives and rewards – such as two non-job search days a week, if you accomplish targets A, B, C, and D.

19. **You should be open-minded and keep an eye open for "luck":** Too much planning can blind you to unexpected and fruitful opportunities. You should welcome serendipity. Learn to re-evaluate your goals and strategies. Seize new opportunities if appropriate.

20. **You should evaluate your progress and adjust:** Take two hours once every two weeks and evaluate your accomplishments. If necessary, tinker with your plans and reorganize your activities and priorities. Don't become too routinized and thereby kill creativity and innovation.

These principles should provide you with an initial orientation for starting your job search. As you become more experienced, you will develop your own set of operating principles that should work for you in particular employment situations.

Make Time for Implementation

One of the most difficult aspects of conducting a job search is finding sufficient time to engage in what one quickly discovers is a very time-consuming set of activities. If you decide to conduct your own job search with minimum assistance from professionals, your major cost will be your time. Therefore, you must find sufficient time to devote to your job search. Ask yourself this question:

"How valuable is my time in relation to finding
a job or changing my career?"

Assign a dollar value to your time. For example, is your time worth $3, $5, $10, $25, $50, or $100 an hour? Compare your figure with what you might pay a professional for doing much of the job search work for you. Normal professional fees range from $1,500 to $10,000.

The time you devote to your job search will depend on whether you want to work at it on a full-time or part-time basis. If you are unemployed, by all means make this a full-time endeavor – 40 to 80 hours per week. If you are presently employed, we do not recommend quitting your job in order to look for employment. You will probably need the steady income and attendant health benefits during your transition period. Furthermore, it is easier to find new employment by appearing employed. Unemployed people project a negative image in the eyes of many employers – they appear to need a job. **Your goal is to find a job based on your strengths rather than your needs.**

However, if you go back to school for skills retraining, your present employment status may be less relevant to employers. In fact, your major strength is the fact that you have acquired a skill the employer needs. If you quit your job and spend money retraining, you will communicate a certain degree of risk-taking, drive, responsibility, and dedication which employers readily seek, but seldom find, in candidates today.

Assuming you will be conducting a job search on a part-time basis – 15 to 25 hours per week – you will need to find the necessary time for these job activities. Unfortunately, most people are busy, having programmed every hour for "important" personal and professional activities. Thus, conducting a job search for 15 or more hours a week means that some things will have to go or receive low priority in relation to your job search.

This is easier said than done. The job search often gets low priority. It competes with other important daily routines, such as attending meetings, taking children to games, going shopping, watching favorite TV programs, and using the Internet. Rather than fight with your routines – and create family disharmony and stress – make your job search part of your daily routines by improving your overall management of time.

Certain time management techniques will help you make your job search a high-priority activity in your daily schedule. These practices may actually lower your present stress level and thus enhance your overall effectiveness.

Time management experts estimate that most people waste their time on unimportant matters. Lacking priorities, people spend 80 percent of their time on trivia and 20 percent of their time on the important matters which should get the most attention. If you reverse this emphasis, you could have a great deal of excess time – and probably experience less stress attendant with the common practice of crisis-managing the critical 20 percent.

Before reorganizing your time, you must know how you normally use your time. Therefore, complete the following exercise to assess your time management behavior. While many of these statements are relevant to individuals in managerial positions, respond to those statements that are most relevant to your employment situation.

Your Time Management Inventory

INSTRUCTIONS: Respond to each statement by circling "yes" or "no," depending on which response better represents your normal pattern of behavior.

1. I have a written set of long, intermediate, and short-range goals for myself (and my family).   Yes   No

2. I have a clear idea of what I will do today at work and at home.   Yes   No

3. I have a clear idea of what I want to accomplish at work this coming week and month.   Yes   No

4. I set priorities and follow through on the most important tasks first.   Yes   No

5. I judge my success by the results I produce in relation to my goals.   Yes   No

6. I use a daily, weekly, and monthly calendar for scheduling appointments and setting work targets.   Yes   No

7. I delegate as much work as possible.   Yes   No

8. I get my subordinates to organize their time in relation to mine.   Yes   No

9. I file only those things which are essential to my work. When in doubt, I throw it out.   Yes   No

10. I throw away junk mail and delete spam.   Yes   No

11. My briefcase is uncluttered, including only essential materials; it serves as my office away from the office.   Yes   No

12. I minimize the number of meetings and con-centrate on making decisions rather than discussing aimlessly.   Yes   No

13. I make frequent use of the telephone and face-to-face encounters rather than written communications. Yes   No

14. I make minor decisions quickly. Yes   No

15. I concentrate on accomplishing one thing at a time. Yes   No

16. I handle each piece of paper once and only once. Yes   No

17. I answer most letters on the letter I receive with either a handwritten or typed message. Yes   No

18. I set deadlines for myself and others and follow through in meeting them. Yes   No

19. I reserve time each week to plan. Yes   No

20. My desk and work area are well organized and clear. Yes   No

21. I know how to say "no" and do so. Yes   No

22. I first skim books, articles, and other forms of written communication for ideas before reading further. Yes   No

23. I monitor my time use during the day by asking myself "How can I best use my time at present?" Yes   No

24. I deal with the present by getting things done that need to be done. Yes   No

25. I maintain a time log to monitor the best use of my time. Yes   No

26. I place a dollar value on my time and behave accordingly. Yes   No

27. I – not others – control my time. Yes   No

28. My briefcase includes items I can work on during spare time in waiting rooms, lines, and airports. Yes   No

29. I keep my door shut when I'm working. Yes   No

30.   I regularly evaluate to what degree I am
       achieving my stated goals.   Yes   No

If you answered "no" to many of these statements, you should consider incorporating a few basic time management principles and practices into your daily schedule. But don't go to extremes by drastically restructuring your life around the "religion" of time management. If you followed all the advice of time management experts, you would probably alienate your family, friends, and colleagues with your narrow efficiency mentality! A realistic approach is to start monitoring your time use and then gradually re-organize your time according to goals and priorities. This is all you need to do. Forget the elaborate flow charts that are the stuff of expensive time management workshops and consultants. Start by developing a time management log that helps you monitor your present use of time. Keep daily records of how you use your time over a two-week period. Identify who controls your time and the results of your time utilization. Within two weeks, clear patterns will emerge. You may learn that you have an "open door" policy that enables others to control your time, leaving little time to do your own work. You may spend too much time on the Internet engaged in wasteful activities. Based on this information, you may need to close your door, be more selective about your choices, and confine meetings, telephone calls, and Internet usage to a particular time of day. You may find from your analysis that you use most time for activities that have few if any important outcomes. If this is the case, then you may need to set goals and prioritize daily activities.

A simple yet effective technique for improving your time management practices is to complete a "to do" list for each day. You can purchase tablets of these forms in many stationery and office supply stores, or you can develop your own "Things To Do Today" list. This list also should prioritize which activities are most important to accomplish each day. Include at the top of your list a particular job search activity or several activities that should be completed on each day. If you follow this simple time management practice, you will find the necessary time to include your job search in your daily routines. You can give your job search top priority. Better still, you will accomplish more in less time, and with better results.

Assess Your Job Search Effectiveness

Just how prepared are you to organize and implement an effective job search? Let's begin by testing for the level of job search information, skills, and strategies you currently possess as well as those you need to develop and improve. Identify your level of job search competence by completing the following exercise:

INSTRUCTIONS: Respond to each statement by circling which number at the right best represents your situation.

SCALE: 1 = strongly agree   4 = disagree
            2 = agree   5 = strongly disagree
            3 = maybe, not certain

1.	I know what motivates me to excel at work.	1 2 3 4 5
2.	I can identify my strongest abilities and skills.	1 2 3 4 5
3.	I have seven major achievements that clarify a pattern of interests and abilities that are relevant to my job and career.	1 2 3 4 5
4.	I know what I both like and dislike in work.	1 2 3 4 5
5.	I know what I want to do during the next 10 years.	1 2 3 4 5
6.	I have a well defined career objective that focuses my job search on particular organizations and employers.	1 2 3 4 5
7.	I know what skills I can offer employers in different occupations.	1 2 3 4 5
8.	I know what skills employers most seek in candidates.	1 2 3 4 5
9.	I can clearly explain to employers what I do well and enjoy doing.	1 2 3 4 5
10.	I can specify why employers should hire me.	1 2 3 4 5

11. I can gain the support of family and friends
    for making a job or career change.   1 2 3 4 5

12. I can find 10 to 20 hours a week to
    conduct a part-time job search.   1 2 3 4 5

13. I have the financial ability to sustain a
    three-month job search.   1 2 3 4 5

14. I can conduct library and interview research
    on different occupations, employers,
    organizations, and communities.   1 2 3 4 5

15. I can write different types of effective
    resumes and job search/thank you letters.   1 2 3 4 5

16. I can produce and distribute resumes and
    letters to the right people.   1 2 3 4 5

17. I can list my major accomplishments in
    action terms.   1 2 3 4 5

18. I can identify and target employers I want
    to interview.   1 2 3 4 5

19. I know how to use the Internet to conduct
    employment research and network.   1 2 3 4 5

20. I know which websites are best for posting
    my resume and browsing job postings.   1 2 3 4 5

21. I know how much time I should spend
    conducting an online job search.   1 2 3 4 5

22. I can develop a job referral network.   1 2 3 4 5

23. I can persuade others to join in forming
    a job search support group.   1 2 3 4 5

24. I can prospect for job leads.   1 2 3 4 5

25. I can use the telephone to develop prospects
    and get referrals and interviews.   1 2 3 4 5

26. I can plan and implement an effective
    direct-mail job search campaign.   1 2 3 4 5

27. I can persuade employers to interview me.   1 2 3 4 5

28. I have a list of at least 10 employer-centered
    questions I need to ask during interviews.   1 2 3 4 5

29. I know the best time to talk about salary
    with an employer.   1 2 3 4 5

30. I know what I want to do with my life over
    the next 10 years.   1 2 3 4 5

31. I have a clear pattern of accomplishments
    which I can explain to employers with
    examples.   1 2 3 4 5

32. I have little difficulty in making cold calls
    and striking up conversations with strangers.   1 2 3 4 5

33. I usually take responsibility for my own
    actions rather than blame other people for
    my situation or circumstances.   1 2 3 4 5

34. I can generate at least one job interview
    for every 10 job search contacts I make.   1 2 3 4 5

35. I can follow up on job interviews.   1 2 3 4 5

36. I can negotiate a salary 10-20% above
    what an employer initially offers.   1 2 3 4 5

37. I can persuade an employer to renegotiate
    my salary after six months on the job.   1 2 3 4 5

38. I can create a position for myself
    in an organization.   1 2 3 4 5

TOTAL [   ]

Calculate your overall potential job search effectiveness by adding the numbers you circled for a composite score. If your total is more than 90 points, you need to work on developing your job search. How you scored each item will indicate to what degree you need to work on improving specific job search skills. If your score is under 60 points, you are well on your way toward job search success.

Attitude Is Key to Success

Maintaining a positive attitude and projecting enthusiasm are extremely important for conducting a successful job search. After all, you are likely to encounter numerous rejections that can discourage you in moving forward with your job search. Check out your attitude by responding to the following statements. Indicate your agreement or disagreement with each statement:

		Yes	No
1.	Other people often make my work difficult.	❏	❏
2.	If I get into trouble, it probably won't be my fault.	❏	❏
3.	I feel people often take advantage of me.	❏	❏
4.	People less qualified than me often get promoted at work.	❏	❏
5.	I avoid taking risks because I'm afraid of failing.	❏	❏
6.	I don't trust many of the people I work with.	❏	❏
7.	Not many people I work with take responsibility.	❏	❏
8.	Most people get ahead because of connections, schmoozing, and office politics.	❏	❏
9.	At work I'm often assigned more than other people in similar positions.	❏	❏
10.	I expect to be discriminated against in the job search and on the job.	❏	❏
11.	I don't feel like I can change many things.	❏	❏
12.	I should have been promoted a long time ago.	❏	❏
13.	I usually have to do the work myself rather than rely on others to get things done.	❏	❏
14.	People often pick on me.	❏	❏

15. Employers try to take advantage of job seekers
    by offering them low salaries.   ❏   ❏

16. I don't like many of the people I work with.   ❏   ❏

17. There's not much I can do to get ahead.   ❏   ❏

18. My ideas are not really taken seriously.   ❏   ❏

19. I often think of reasons why my boss's and
    co-workers' ideas won't work.   ❏   ❏

20. I sometimes respond to suggestions by saying
    *"Yes, but...," "I'm not sure...," "I don't think
    it will work...," "Let's not do that..."*   ❏   ❏

21. Customers are often wrong but I have to put
    up with them nonetheless.   ❏   ❏

22. I don't see why I need to go for more training.   ❏   ❏

23. I often wish my boss would just disappear.   ❏   ❏

24. I sometimes feel depressed at work.   ❏   ❏

25. I have a hard time getting motivated at work.   ❏   ❏

26. I don't look forward to going to work on Monday.   ❏   ❏

27. Friday is my favorite workday.   ❏   ❏

28. I sometimes come to work late or leave early.   ❏   ❏

29. My current job doesn't reflect my true talents.   ❏   ❏

30. I should have advanced a lot further in my career
    than my current position and salary indicate.   ❏   ❏

31. I'm worth a lot more than most employers
    are willing to pay.   ❏   ❏

32. I sometimes do things behind my boss's back
    that could get me into trouble.   ❏   ❏

TOTALS   ____   ____

Not all of these statements necessarily reflect bad attitudes. Some may be honest assessments of how a company operates in practice. Indeed, some organizations have dysfunctional environments that breed negative attitudes. However, if you checked "Yes" to more than six of the statements, chances are you may be harboring some bad attitudes that affect both your job search and your on-the-job performance. You may want to examine these attitudes as possible barriers to getting ahead in your job search as well as on the job.

Excuses for Dysfunctional Behavior

Many negative attitudes relate to excuses we make for dysfunctional behavior. Take, for example, the following condensed list (reduced from 100 to 48) of excuses compiled by Rory Donaldson on www.brainsarefun.com that often relate to the workplace:

1. It's your fault.
2. I'm not happy.
3. It's too hot.
4. I'm too busy.
5. I'm sad.
6. I didn't sleep well.
7. It's not fair.
8. I didn't write it down.
9. It's too hard.
10. I forgot.
11. There was too much traffic.
12. I tried.
13. I didn't know it was today.
14. I'm too tired.
15. I thought it was due tomorrow.
16. I ran out of time.
17. I don't feel well.
18. You didn't tell me.
19. I'm not good at that.
20. I was rushed.
21. You didn't give it to me.
22. We did that last year.
23. That's not the way we learned at school.
24. I already did it.
25. It was right here.
26. It's too much work.
27. I was frustrated.
28. I did already.
29. I lost it.
30. Nobody likes me.
31. I have poor self esteem.
32. I'm too happy.
33. I'm sleepy.
34. I already know that.
35. It's too easy.
36. It's not important.
37. I have a learning disorder.
38. I have a different learning style.
39. I didn't know.
40. I don't have to.
41. I don't know how.
42. I can't.
43. I don't know where it is.
44. I'm too stupid.
45. You lost it.
46. It takes too much time.
47. He told me I didn't have to.
48. I'm doing something else.

Here are 20 additional excuses we and others have frequently encountered in the workplace. Some are even used by candidates during a
job interview to explain their on-the-job behavior – killer attitudes that
may ensure never being offered the job! Most of these excuses reflect an
attitude lacking in responsibility and initiative:

1. No one told me.	11. I don't know how to do it.
2. I did what you said.	12. That's your problem.
3. Your directions were bad.	13. It wasn't very good.
4. It's not my fault.	14. Maybe you did it.
5. She did it.	15. I thought I wrote it down.
6. It just seemed to happen.	16. That's not my style.
7. It happens a lot.	17. He told me to do it that way.
8. What did he say?	18. I've got to go now.
9. I had a headache.	19. Where do you think it went?
10. I don't understand why.	20. We can talk about it later.

People with a positive attitude and proactive behavior don't engage in
behaviors that reflect such excuses. They have a "can do" attitude that
helps focus their goals on doing those things that are most important to
achieving their goals. For example, rather than show up 10 minutes late
for a job interview and say they got lost or had bad directions, people
with a positive attitude and proactive behavior scope out the interview
location the day before in anticipation of arriving 10 minutes early. They
make no excuses because they engage in no-excuses behavior!

Changing Negative Attitudes

If you have negative attitudes and often need to make excuses for your
behavior, it's time you took control of both your attitudes and behaviors.
Begin by identifying several of your negative attitudes and try to transform them into positive attitudes. For starters, examine these sets of
negative and positive attitudes that can arise at various stages of the job
search, especially during the critical job interview:

Negative Attitude	Positive Attitude
I didn't like my last employer.	It was time for me to move on to a more progressive company.
I haven't been able to find a job in over three months. I really want this one.	I've been learning a great deal during the past several weeks of my job search.

My last three jobs were problems.	I learned a great deal about what I really love to do from those last three jobs.
Do you have a job?	I'm in the process of conducting a job search. Do you know anyone who might have an interest in someone with my qualifications?
I can't come in for an interview tomorrow since I'm interviewing for another job. What about Wednesday? That looks good.	I have a conflict tomorrow. Wednesday would be good. Could we do something in the morning?
Yes, I flunked out of college in my sophomore year.	After two years in college I decided to pursue a career in computer sales.
I really hated studying math.	Does this job require math?
Sorry about that spelling error on my resume. I was never good at spelling.	(Doesn't point it out; if asked, say *"I'm embarrassed. That one got away!"*)
I don't enjoy working in teams.	I work best when given an assignment that allows me to work on my own.
What does this job pay?	How does the pay scale here compare with other firms in the area?
Will I have to work weekends?	What are the normal hours for someone in this position?
I have to see my psychiatrist once a month. Can I have that day off?	I have an appointment I need to keep the last Friday of each month. Would it be okay if I took off three hours that day?
I'm three months pregnant. Will your health care program cover my delivery?	Could you tell me more about your benefits, such as health and dental care?

Can you think of any particular negative attitudes you might have that you can restate in positive language? Identify five that relate to your job search and work. Present them in both the negative and positive:

Negative Attitude	**Positive Attitude**
1. _____	_____
_____	_____
_____	_____
2. _____	_____
_____	_____
_____	_____
3. _____	_____
_____	_____
_____	_____
4. _____	_____
_____	_____
_____	_____
5. _____	_____
_____	_____
_____	_____

Effective Resumes and Letters

Your resumes and letters are your calling cards for getting job interviews. Similar to a good advertisement, they need to move the reader to take action – invite you to an interview. However, many resumes are literally "dead upon arrival" because the job seeker made serious writing and distribution errors. Employers frequently report the following common resume mistakes candidates make which often eliminate them from competition. Most of these mistakes center on issues of focus, organization, trustworthiness, intelligence, and competence. Reading between the lines, employers often draw conclusions about the individual's personality and competence based upon the number of errors found on the resume.

Deadly Errors

If you make any of these errors, chances are your **credibility** will be called into question. Make sure your resume does not commit any of these writing errors:

1. Unrelated to the position in question.
2. Too long or too short.
3. Unattractive with a poorly designed format, small type style, and crowded copy.
4. Misspellings, poor grammar, wordiness, and redundancy.
5. Punctuation errors.
6. Lengthy phrases, long sentences, and awkward paragraphs.
7. Slick, amateurish, or "gimmicky" – appears over-produced.
8. Boastful, egocentric, and aggressive.
9. Dishonest, untrustworthy, or suspicious information.
10. Missing critical categories, such as experience, skills, and education.
11. Difficult to interpret because of poor organization and lack of focus; unclear what the person has done or can do.
12. Unexplained time gaps between jobs.
13. Too many jobs in a short period of time – a job hopper with little evidence of career advancement.
14. No evidence of past accomplishments or a pattern of performance from which to predict future performance. Primarily focuses on formal duties and responsibilities that came with previous jobs.
15. Lacks credibility and content – includes a great deal of fluff and "canned" resume language.
16. States a strange, unclear, or vague objective.
17. Appears over-qualified or under-qualified for the position.
18. Includes distracting personal information that does not enhance the resume nor candidacy.
19. Fails to include critical contact information (telephone number and e-mail address) and uses an anonymous address (P.O. Box number).
20. Uses jargon and abbreviations unfamiliar to the reader.
21. Embellishes name with formal titles, middle names, and nicknames which make him or her appear odd or strange.

22. Repeatedly refers to "I" and appears self-centered.
23. Includes obvious self-serving references that raise credibility questions.
24. Sloppy, with handwritten corrections – crosses out "married" and writes "single"!
25. Includes "red flag" information such as being fired, lawsuits or claims, health or performance problems, or starting salary figures, including salary requirements that may be too high or too low.

Assuming you have written a great resume and a very persuasive cover letter, your next challenge is to make sure you don't make several errors relating to the production, distribution, and follow-up stages of your resumes and letters. Here are some of the most common such errors you must avoid:

1. Poorly typed and reproduced – hard to read.
2. Produced on odd-sized paper.
3. Printed on poor quality paper or on extremely thin or thick paper.
4. Soiled with coffee stains, fingerprints, or ink marks.
5. Sent to the wrong person or department.
6. Mailed, faxed, or e-mailed to "To Whom It May Concern" or "Dear Sir."
7. E-mailed as an attachment which could have a virus if opened.
8. Enclosed in a tiny envelope that requires the resume to be unfolded and flattened several times.
9. Arrived without proper postage – employer must pay the extra!
10. Sent the resume and letter by the slowest postage rate possible.
11. Envelope double-sealed with tape and is indestructible – nearly impossible to open by conventional means!
12. Back of envelope includes a handwritten note stating that something is missing on the resume, such as a telephone number, e-mail address, or new mailing address.
13. Resume taped to the inside of the envelope, an old European habit practiced by paranoid letter writers. Need to destroy the envelope and perhaps the resume as well to get it out.

14. Accompanied by extraneous or inappropriate enclosures which were not requested, such as copies of self-serving letters or recommendations, transcripts, or samples of work.
15. Arrives too late for consideration.
16. Comes without a cover letter.
17. Cover letter repeats what's on the resumes – does not command attention nor move the reader to action.
18. Sent the same or different versions of the resume to the same person as a seemingly clever follow-up method.
19. Follow-up call made too soon – before the resume and letter arrive!
20. Follow-up call is too aggressive or the candidate appears too "hungry" for the position – appears needy or greedy.

Evaluate the Final Product

Once you complete your resume, be sure to evaluate it. You should do this by conducting two evaluations: internal and external. With an **internal evaluation**, you assess your resume in reference to specific self-evaluation criteria. An **external evaluation** involves having someone else critique your resume for its overall effectiveness. The following evaluation instruments reflect many of the best principles for writing, producing, distribution, and following up resumes.

Internal Evaluation

The first evaluation should take place immediately upon completing the first draft of your resume. Examine your resume in reference to the following criteria. Respond to each statement by circling the appropriate number at the right that most accurately describes your resume:

1 = strongly agree	4 = disagree
2 = agree	5 = strongly disagree
3 = neutral	

Writing

1. Wrote the resume myself – no creative plagiarizing from resume examples produced by other people.   1   2   3   4   5

2. Conducted a thorough self-assessment
    which became the basis for writing each
    resume section.   1   2   3   4   5

4. Have a plan of action that relates my
    resume to other job search activities.   1   2   3   4   5

5. Selected an appropriate resume format
    that best presents my interests, skills,
    and experience.   1   2   3   4   5

6. Included all essential information
    categories in the proper order.   1   2   3   4   5

7. Eliminated all extraneous information
    unrelated to my objective and employers'
    needs (date, picture, race, religion, age,
    political affiliation, sex, height, weight,
    marital status, health, hobbies) or better
    saved for discussion in the interview
    (salary history and references).   1   2   3   4   5

8. Put the most important information first.   1   2   3   4   5

9. Resume is oriented to the future rather
    than to the past.   1   2   3   4   5

10. Contact information is complete – name,
    address, and phone number. No P.O.
    Box numbers or nicknames.   1   2   3   4   5

11. Limited abbreviations to a few commonly
    accepted words.   1   2   3   4   5

12. Contact information attractively
    formatted to introduce the resume.   1   2   3   4   5

13. Included a thoughtful employer-oriented
    objective that incorporates both skills
    and benefits.   1   2   3   4   5

14. Objective clearly communicates to
    employers what I want to do, can do,
    and will do for them.   1   2   3   4   5

15. Objective is neither too general nor
    too specific.   1   2   3   4   5

16. Objective serves as the central organizing element for all other sections of the resume.   1   2   3   4   5

17. Considered including a "Summary of Qualifications" section.   1   2   3   4   5

18. Elaborated work experience in detail, emphasizing my skills, abilities, and achievements.   1   2   3   4   5

19. Each "Experience" section is short and to the point.   1   2   3   4   5

20. Consistently used action verbs and the active voice.   1   2   3   4   5

21. Incorporated language appropriate for the keywords of electronic resume scanners.   1   2   3   4   5

22. Did not refer to myself as "I."   1   2   3   4   5

23. Used specifics – numbers and percentages – to highlight my performance.   1   2   3   4   5

24. Included positive quotations about my performance from previous employers.   1   2   3   4   5

25. Eliminated any negative references, including reasons for leaving.   1   2   3   4   5

26. Did not include names of supervisors.   1   2   3   4   5

27. Summarized my most recent job and then included other jobs in reverse chronological order.   1   2   3   4   5

28. Descriptions of "Experience" are consistent.   1   2   3   4   5

29. Put the most important information about my skills first when summarizing my "Experience."   1   2   3   4   5

30. No time gaps nor "job hopping" apparent to reader.   1   2   3   4   5

31. Documented "other experience" that might strengthen my objective and decided to either include or exclude it on the resume.   1   2   3   4   5

32. Included complete information on my educational background, including important highlights.   1   2   3   4   5

33. If a recent graduate with little relevant work experience, emphasized educational background more than work experience.   1   2   3   4   5

34. Put education in reverse chronological order and eliminated high school if a college graduate.   1   2   3   4   5

35. Included special education and training relevant to my major interests and skills.   1   2   3   4   5

36. Included professional affiliations and membership relevant to my objective and skills; highlighted any major contributions.   1   2   3   4   5

37. Documented any special skills not included elsewhere on resume and included those that appear relevant to employers' needs.   1   2   3   4   5

38. Included awards or special recognitions that further document my skills and achievements.   1   2   3   4   5

39. Weighed the pros and cons of including a personal statement on my resume.   1   2   3   4   5

40. Did not mention salary history or expectations.   1   2   3   4   5

41. Did not include names, addresses, and phone numbers of references.   1   2   3   4   5

42. Included additional information to enhance the interest of employers.   1   2   3   4   5

43. Used language appropriate for the employer, including terms that associate me with the industry.   1   2   3   4   5

44. My language is crisp, succinct, expressive, and direct.   1 2 3 4 5

45. Used highlighting and emphasizing techniques to make the resume most readable to the individual (a conventional resume); avoided such elements when writing an electronic or scannable resume.   1 2 3 4 5

46. Selected language that is appropriate for being "read" by today's resume scanning technology.   1 2 3 4 5

47. Resume has an inviting, uncluttered look incorporating sufficient white space and using a standard type style and size.   1 2 3 4 5

48. Kept the design very basic and conservative.   1 2 3 4 5

49. Kept sentences and sections short and succinct.   1 2 3 4 5

50. Resume runs one or two pages.   1 2 3 4 5

Production

51. Carefully proofread and produced two or three drafts which were subjected to both internal and external evaluations before producing the final copies.   1 2 3 4 5

52. Chose a standard color and paper quality.   1 2 3 4 5

53. Used 8½" x 11" paper.   1 2 3 4 5

54. Printed resume on only one side of paper.   1 2 3 4 5

55. Used a good quality printer and an easy-to-read typeface.   1 2 3 4 5

Marketing and Distribution

56. Targeted resume toward specific employers.   1 2 3 4 5

57. Used resume properly for networking and informational interviewing activities.   1 2 3 4 5

58. Considered entering resume into online
    resume databases and responding to job
    listings found on several Internet
    employment sites.   1   2   3   4   5

59. Resume accompanied by a dynamite
    cover letter.   1   2   3   4   5

60. Only enclosed a cover letter with my
    resume – nothing else.   1   2   3   4   5

61. Addressed to a specific name and
    position.   1   2   3   4   5

62. Mailed resume and cover letter in a
    matching No. 10 business envelope
    or in a 9" x 12" envelope.   1   2   3   4   5

63. Typed address on envelope.   1   2   3   4   5

64. Sent correspondence by first-class or
    priority mail or special next-day services;
    affixed attractive commemorative
    stamps.   1   2   3   4   5

Follow-Up

65. Followed up the mailed resume
    within 7 days.   1   2   3   4   5

66. Used the telephone for following up.   1   2   3   4   5

67. Followed up the follow-up with a nice
    thank-you letter.   1   2   3   4   5

TOTAL

Add the numbers you circled to the right of each statement to get a cumulative score. If your score is higher than 90, you need to work on improving various aspects of your resume. Go back and institute the necessary changes to create a truly dynamite resume.

External Evaluation

In many respects the external resume evaluation plays the most crucial role in your overall job search. It helps you get remembered, which, in turn, may lead to referrals and job leads.

The best way to conduct an external evaluation is to show your resume to two or more individuals. Choose people whose opinions you value for being objective, frank, and thoughtful. Do not select friends and relatives who might flatter you with positive comments. Professional acquaintances or people you don't know personally but whom you admire may be good candidates for this type of evaluation.

An ideal evaluator has experience in hiring people in your area of expertise. In addition to sharing their experience with you, they may refer you to other individuals who would be interested in your qualifications. You will encounter many of these individuals in the process of networking and conducting informational interviews. You, in effect, conduct an external evaluation of your resume with this individual during the informational interview. At the very end of the informational interview you should ask the person to examine your resume; you want to elicit comments on how you can better strengthen the resume. Ask the following questions:

"If you don't mind, would you look over my resume? Perhaps you could comment on its clarity or make suggestions for improving it?"

"How would you react to this resume if you received it from a candidate? Does it grab your attention and interest you enough to talk with me?"

"If you were writing this resume, what changes would you make? Any additions, deletions, or modifications?"

Answers to these questions should give you valuable feedback for improving both the form and content of your resume. You will be eliciting advice from people whose opinions count. However, it is not necessary to incorporate all such advice. Some evaluators, while well-meaning, will not provide you with sound advice. Instead, they may reinforce many of the pitfalls found in weak resumes.

Another way to conduct an external evaluation is to develop a checklist of evaluation criteria and give it, along with your resume, to individuals whose opinions and expertise you value. Unlike the self-evaluation criteria used for the internal evaluation, the evaluation criteria for the external evaluation should be more general. Examine your resume in relation to these criteria:

INSTRUCTIONS: Circle the number that best characterizes various aspects of your resume as well as include any recommendations on how to best improve the resume:

1 = excellent   2 = okay   3 = weak

Recommendations
for improvement

1.	Overall appearance	1	2	3	_____
2.	Layout	1	2	3	_____
3.	Clarity	1	2	3	_____
4.	Consistency	1	2	3	_____
5.	Readability	1	2	3	_____
6.	Language	1	2	3	_____
7.	Organization	1	2	3	_____
8.	Content/completeness	1	2	3	_____
9.	Length	1	2	3	_____
10.	Contact info/header	1	2	3	_____
11.	Objective	1	2	3	_____
12.	Experience	1	2	3	_____
13.	Skills	1	2	3	_____
14.	Achievements	1	2	3	_____
15.	Education	1	2	3	_____
16.	Other information	1	2	3	_____
17.	Paper color	1	2	3	_____
18.	Paper size and stock	1	2	3	_____
19.	Overall production quality	1	2	3	_____
20.	Potential effectiveness	1	2	3	_____

SUMMARY EVALUATION: _____

_____

_____

After completing these external evaluations and incorporating useful suggestions for further improving the quality of your resume, it's a good idea to send a copy of your revised resume to those individuals who were helpful in giving you advice. Thank them for their time and thoughtful comments. Ask them to keep you in mind should they hear of anyone who might be interested in your experience and skills. In so doing, you will be demonstrating your appreciation and thoughtfulness as well as reminding them to remember you for further information, advice, and referrals.

In the end, **being remembered in reference to your resume** is one of the most important goals you want to repeatedly achieve during your job search. As you will quickly discover, your most effective job search strategy involves networking with your resume. You want to share information, by way of the informational interview, about your interests and qualifications with those who can give advice, know about job vacancies, or can refer you to individuals who have the power to hire. Your resume, and especially this external evaluation, plays a critical role in furthering this process.

Whatever you do, make sure you write, produce, and distribute error-free resumes and letters. If you commit any of the above errors, chances are you will be eliminated from consideration or your candidacy will be greatly diminished.

Useful Resources

If you need assistance in writing, producing, and distributing your resume and letters, we recommend the following books:

> *101 Best Resumes* (Jay Block and Michael Betrus)
> *175 High-Impact Cover Letters* (Richard Beatty)
> *175 High-Impact Resumes* (Richard Beatty)
> *201 Dynamite Job Search Letters* (Ron and Caryl Krannich)
> *America's Top Resumes for America's Top Jobs* (J. Michael Farr)

Best Cover Letters for $100,000+ Jobs (Wendy S. Enelow)

Best KeyWords for Resumes, Cover Letters, and Interviews (Wendy S. Enelow)

Best Resumes and CVs for International Jobs (Ronald L. Krannich and Wendy S. Enelow)

Best Resumes for $75,000+ College Grads (Wendy S. Enelow)

Best Resumes for $100,000+ Jobs (Wendy S. Enelow)

Best Resumes for People Without a Four-Year Degree (Wendy S. Enelow)

Cover Letters That Knock 'em Dead (Martin Yate)

Cover Letters for Dummies (Joyce Lain Kennedy)

Cyberspace Resume Kit (Fred Jandt and Mary Nemnich)

Electronic Resumes and Online Networking (Rebecca Smith)

e-Resumes (Susan Britton Whitcomb and Pat Kendall)

Expert Resumes for People Returning to Work (Wendy S. Enelow and Louise M. Kursmark)

Gallery of Best Cover Letters (David F. Noble)

Gallery of Best Resumes (David F. Noble)

Haldane's Best Cover Letters for Professionals (Bernard Haldane Associates)

Haldane's Best Resumes for Professionals (Bernard Haldane Associates)

High Impact Resumes and Letters (Ronald L. Krannich and William J. Banis)

Military Resumes and Cover Letters (Carl S. Savino and Ronald L. Krannich)

Nail the Cover Letter! (Ron and Caryl Krannich)

Nail the Resume! (Ron and Caryl Krannich)

Power Resumes (Ron Tepper)

Resumes for Dummies (Joyce Lain Kennedy)

Resumes in Cyberspace (Pat Criscito)

Resumes That Knock 'Em Dead (Martin Yate)

The Savvy Resume Writer (Ron and Caryl Krannich)

Several software programs assist individuals in quickly producing resumes that follow standard computer-generated formats. Two of the most popular such programs include:

ResumeMaker
WinWay Resume Deluxe 10.0

Several websites provide useful tips on how to write resumes and letters:

- **Monster.com**   http://resume.monster.com
- **America's CareerInfoNet**   www.acinet.org/acinet
- **JobStar**   www.jobstar.org/tools/resume
- **CareerBuilder**   www.careerbuilder.com
- **Career Journal**   www.careerjournal.com/job
                                 hunting/resumes
- **Quintessential Careers**   www.quintcareers.com
- **Wetfeet**   www.wetfeet.com
- **WinningTheJob**   www.winningthejob.com

A few sites, such as www.vault.com, even provide a free online resume review by a career professional. Other sites, such as www.careerbuilder. com ("Advice & Resources") and www.flipdog.com ("Resource Center"), primarily include sponsored links to companies that offer fee-based resume writing and distribution services. Resume writing professionals, such as author Rebecca Smith, maintain their own websites (www. eresumes.com) with tips on writing an electronic resume.

If you feel you could benefit from the services of a professional resume writer, expect to pay between $100 to $500 for a resume, and check out these websites for assistance:

- **Professional Association of Resume
  Writers and Career Coaches**   www,parw.com
- **Professional Resume Writing
  and Research Association**   www.prwra.com
- **National Resume Writers'
  Association**   www.nrwa.com

A Google.com or Yahoo.com search for "resume writers" or "directory professional resume writers" will yield dozens of professional resume writing firms and individuals who offer a variety of resume and letter production services. Some also include distribution services along with related job search services, such as interview coaching. If you review several of these websites, you'll get a very good idea of the range and costs of such career-related services.

Resume distribution approaches and services have always been controversial, whether offline or online. Indeed, career counselors usually caution job seekers about literally "throwing money to the wind" by shotgunning, or blasting, their resumes to hundreds of employers. This approach usually gives job seekers a false sense of hope – they feel they are actually doing something to advance their job search by reaching out by mail or e-mail to literally touch potential employers! However, this is usually the approach of unfocused, and often desperate and unrealistic, job seekers. As the Internet increasingly plays an important role in the job search, several companies now specialize in blasting resumes via e-mail to hundreds individuals possibly interested in receiving such resumes. For a fee ranging from $19.95 to $199.95, they will e-mail your resume to a special list of executive recruiters and employers, but primarily to executive recruiters. We're very dubious about this approach, despite many self-serving testimonials to the contrary. You'll probably get what you pay for using this borderline spam approach to resume distribution – little to nothing and lots of false hopes. If you're interested in trying your luck with this approach, check out these resume blasting sites which include information on their services:

- **BlastMyResume**   www.blastmyresume.com
- **Careerxpress.com**   www.careerxpress.com
- **E-cv.com**   www.e-cv.com
- **ExecutiveAgent.com**   www.executiveagent.com
- **HotResumes.com**   www.hotresumes.com
- **Job Village**   www.jobvillage.com
- **Resume Agent**   www.resumeagent.com
- **ResumeBlaster**   www.resumeblaster.com
- **Resume Booster**   www.resumebooster.com
- **ResumeBroadcaster**   www.resumebroadcaster.com
- **Resume Machine**   www.resumemachine.com
- **Resume Rabbit**   www.resumerabbit.com
                               (posts to multiple job boards)
- **ResumeZapper**   www.resumezapper.com
- **ResumeXpress**   www.resumexpress.com

- RocketResume   www.rocketresume.com
- SeeMeResumes.com   www.seemeresumes.com
- WSACORP.com   www.wsacorp.com

Network Your Way to Job Success

Networking is the key to finding good quality jobs. Rather than spend most of your time posting resumes to websites and responding to classified ads and job announcements, you are well advised to develop an effective networking campaign that connects you to unadvertised jobs on the hidden job market and to the right people who have the power to hire for such jobs. The process of networking involves **connecting, building, and nurturing networks of relationships** that generate three critical components in an effective job search – information, advice, and referrals. A vigorous networking campaign quickly snowballs information, advice, and referrals into job leads, interviews, and offers. As we noted in Chapter 3 (pages 38-42), as well as in our separate treatment of the networking process *(The Savvy Networker: Building Your Job Net for Success*, Impact Publications), networking can take both offline and online forms.

Just how savvy are you when it comes to finding a job and advancing your career? Do you have the necessary networking skills for success? Can you quickly network your way to job and career success, or do you need to focus on developing specific networking skills? Let's identify "Your Savvy Networking I.Q." You do this by responding to the following set of agree/disagree statements that relate to your networking skills:

Your Savvy Networking I.Q.

INSTRUCTIONS: Respond to each statement by circling the number to the right that best represents your situation. The higher your score, the higher your "Savvy Networking IQ."

SCALE: 5 = strongly agree   2 = disagree
           4 = agree   1 = strongly disagree
           3 = maybe, not certain

1. I enjoy going to business and social
    functions where I have an opportunity to
    meet new people. (CONNECT/BUILD)   5 4 3 2 1

2. I usually take the initiative in introducing
    myself to people I don't know. (CONNECT)   5 4 3 2 1

3. I enjoy being in groups and actively
    participating in group activities.
    (CONNECT/BUILD)   5 4 3 2 1

4. On a scale of 1 to 10, my social skills
    are at least a "9." (BUILD/NURTURE)   5 4 3 2 1

5. I listen carefully and give positive
    feedback when someone is speaking
    to me. (CONNECT/BUILD)   5 4 3 2 1

6. I have a friendly and engaging
    personality that attracts others to me.
    (CONNECT/BUILD/NURTURE)   5 4 3 2 1

7. I make a special effort to remember
    people's names and frequently address
    them by their name. (CONNECT)   5 4 3 2 1

8. I carry business cards and often give
    them to acquaintances from whom I
    also collect business cards. (CONNECT)   5 4 3 2 1

9. I have a system for organizing business
    cards I receive, including notes on the
    back of each card. (BUILD)   5 4 3 2 1

10. I seldom have a problem starting a
    conversation and engaging in small
    talk with strangers. (CONNECT)   5 4 3 2 1

11. I enjoy making cold calls and persuading
    strangers to meet with me. (CONNECT)   5 4 3 2 1

12. I usually return phone calls in a timely
    manner. (CONNECT)   5 4 3 2 1

13. If I can't get through to someone on the
    phone, I'll keep trying until I do, even if it
    means making 10 more calls. (CONNECT)   5 4 3 2 1

14. I follow up on new contacts by phone,
    e-mail, or letter. (BUILD)   5 4 3 2 1

15. I have several friends who will give me
    job leads. (BUILD)   5 4 3 2 1

16. I frequently give and receive referrals.
    (BUILD)   5 4 3 2 1

17. I have many friends. (BUILD)   5 4 3 2 1

18. I know at least 25 people who can give
    me career advice and referrals. (BUILD)   5 4 3 2 1

19. I don't mind approaching people with my
    professional concerns. (CONNECT/BUILD)   5 4 3 2 1

20. I enjoy having others contribute to my
    success. (BUILD)   5 4 3 2 1

21. When I have a problem or face a
    challenge, I usually contact someone
    for information and advice. (BUILD)   5 4 3 2 1

22. I'm good at asking questions and getting
    useful advice from others. (BUILD)   5 4 3 2 1

23. I usually handle rejections in stride by
    learning from them and moving on.
    (BUILD)   5 4 3 2 1

24. I can sketch a diagram, with appropriate
    linkages, of individuals who are most
    important in both my personal and
    professional networks. (BUILD)   5 4 3 2 1

25. I regularly do online networking by
    participating in Usenet newsgroups,
    mailing lists, chats, and bulletin boards.
    (CONNECT/BUILD)   5 4 3 2 1

26. I regularly communicate my
    accomplishments to key members
    of my network. (NURTURE)   5 4 3 2 1

27. I make it a habit to stay in touch with
    members of my network by telephone,
    e-mail, and letter. (NURTURE)   5 4 3 2 1

28. I regularly send personal notes, birthday
    and holiday greeting cards, and letters
    on special occasions to people in my
    network. (NURTURE)   5 4 3 2 1

29. I still stay in touch with childhood
    friends and old schoolmates. (NURTURE)   5 4 3 2 1

30. I have a great network of individuals
    whom I can call on at anytime for
    assistance, and they will be happy to
    help me. (BUILD/NURTURE)   5 4 3 2 1

31. I belong to several organizations,
    including a professional association.
    (CONNECT/BUILD)   5 4 3 2 1

32. I consider myself an effective networker
    who never abuses his relationships.
    (CONNECT/BUILD/NURTURE)   5 4 3 2 1

33. Others see me as a savvy networker.
    (CONNECT/BUILD/NURTURE)   5 4 3 2 1

TOTAL I.Q.

If your total composite I.Q. is above 155, you're most likely a savvy networker. If you're below 120, you're probably lacking key networking skills. Each of the above items indicates a particular connect, build, or nurture behavior or skill that contributes to one's overall networking effectiveness. Concentrate on improving those skills on which you appear to be weak. For example, you may discover you are particularly savvy at "connecting" with people, but you're weak on "building" and "nurturing" relationships – or vice versa – that define your network.

What's Your Interview I.Q.?

While effective resumes, letters, and networking are keys to getting job interviews, you must perform well in the interview to get the job offer. Just how well prepared are you for the job interview? Respond to the following statements by indicating your degree of agreement with each:

SCALE: 5 = strongly agree   2 = disagree
              4 = agree   1 = strongly disagree
              3 = maybe, not certain

1. I know what skills I can offer employers.   5 4 3 2 1

2. I know what skills employers most seek
    in candidates.   5 4 3 2 1

3. I can clearly explain to employers what
    I do well and enjoy doing.   5 4 3 2 1

4. I can explain in 60 seconds why an
    employer should hire me.   5 4 3 2 1

5. I can identify and target employers
    I want to get an interview with.   5 4 3 2 1

6. I can develop a job referral network.   5 4 3 2 1

7. I can prospect for job leads.   5 4 3 2 1

8. I can generate at least one job interview
    for every 10 job search contacts I make.   5 4 3 2 1

9. I can follow up on job interviews.   5 4 3 2 1

10. I can persuade an employer to renegotiate
    my salary after six months on the job.   5 4 3 2 1

11. I know which questions interviewers are
    most likely to ask me.   5 4 3 2 1

12. If asked to reveal my weaknesses, I know how
    to respond – answer honestly, but always
    stress my strengths.   5 4 3 2 1

13. I know how to best dress for the interview.   5 4 3 2 1

14. I know the various types of interviews I may
    encounter and how to appropriately respond
    in each situation.   5 4 3 2 1

15. I can easily approach strangers for job
    information and advice.   5 4 3 2 1

16. I know where to find information on organizations that are most likely to be interested in my skills.   5 4 3 2 1

17. I know how to go beyond vacancy announcements to locate job opportunities appropriate for my qualifications.   5 4 3 2 1

18. I know how to interview appropriate people for job information and advice.   5 4 3 2 1

19. I know many people who can refer me to others for informational interviews.   5 4 3 2 1

20. I can uncover jobs on the hidden job market.   5 4 3 2 1

21. I know how to prepare and practice for the critical job interview.   5 4 3 2 1

22. I know how to stress my positives.   5 4 3 2 1

23. I know how to research the organization and individuals who are likely to interview me.   5 4 3 2 1

24. I have considered how I would respond to illegal questions posed by prospective employers.   5 4 3 2 1

25. I can telephone effectively for job leads.   5 4 3 2 1

26. I am prepared to conduct an effective telephone interview.   5 4 3 2 1

27. I know when and how to deal with salary questions.   5 4 3 2 1

28. I know what to read while waiting in the outer office prior to the interview.   5 4 3 2 1

29. I can nonverbally communicate my interest and enthusiasm for the job.   5 4 3 2 1

30. I know the best time to arrive at the interview site.   5 4 3 2 1

31. I know how to respond using positive form and content as well as supports when responding to interviewers' questions.   5 4 3 2 1

32. I know how to summarize my strengths
    and value at the closing of the interview.   5 4 3 2 1

33. I know what to include in a thank-you letter.   5 4 3 2 1

34. I know when and how to follow up the
    job interview.   5 4 3 2 1

35. I know what do during the 24- to 48-hour
    period following a job offer.   5 4 3 2 1

36. I can clearly explain to interviewers what
    I like and dislike about particular jobs.   5 4 3 2 1

37. I can explain to interviewers why I made
    my particular educational choices, including
    my major and grade point average.   5 4 3 2 1

38. I can clearly explain to interviewers what
    I want to be doing 5 or 10 years from now.   5 4 3 2 1

39. I have a list of references who can speak in
    a positive manner about me and my work
    abilities.   5 4 3 2 1

40. I can clearly state my job and career
    objectives as both skills and outcomes.   5 4 3 2 1

41. I have set aside 20 hours a week to primarily
    conduct informational interviews.   5 4 3 2 1

42. I know what foods and drinks are best to
    select if the interview includes a luncheon
    or dinner meeting.   5 4 3 2 1

43. I know how to listen effectively.   5 4 3 2 1

44. I can explain why an employer should hire me.   5 4 3 2 1

45. I am prepared to handle the salary question
    at whatever point it comes up.   5 4 3 2 1

46. I know when to use my resume in an informa-
    tional interview.   5 4 3 2 1

47. I can generate three new job leads each day.   5 4 3 2 1

48. I can outline my major achievements in my last three jobs and show how they relate to the job I am interviewing for.   5 4 3 2 1

49. I know what the interviewer is looking for when he or she asks about my weaknesses.   5 4 3 2 1

50. I am prepared to handle panel, serial, stress, behavioral, and situational interviews.   5 4 3 2 1

TOTAL I.Q.   [ ]

Once you have completed this exercise, add your responses to compute a total score. This will be your composite I.Q. If your score is between 200 and 250, you seem well prepared to successfully handle the interview. If your score is between 150 and 199, you are heading in the right direction, and many of our recommended resources should help you increase your interview competencies. If your score falls below 150, you have a great deal of work to do in preparation for the job interview.

If you need help in preparing for the job interview, we recommend the following resources:

Books

101 Dynamite Questions to Ask at Your Job Interview (Richard Fein)

101 Great Answers to the Toughest Interview Questions (Ron Fry)

250 Job Interview Questions You'll Most Likely Be Asked (Peter Veruki)

Adams Job Interview Almanac, with CD-ROM (Adams Media)

Haldane's Best Answers to Tough Interview Questions (Bernard Haldane Associates)

Interview Rehearsal Book (Deb Gottesman and Buzz Mauro)

Job Interview Tips for People With Not-So-Hot Backgrounds (Ron and Caryl Krannich)

Job Interviews for Dummies (Joyce Lain Kennedy)

KeyWords to Nail Your Job Interview (Wendy S. Enelow)

Nail the Job Interview (Caryl and Ron Krannich)

Naked at the Interview (Burton Jay Nadler)

The Perfect Interview (John Drake)

Power Interviews (Neil M. Yeager and Lee Hough)
Savvy Interviewing (Ron and Caryl Krannich)

Websites

- Monster.com   www.interview.monster.com
- InterviewPro   www.interviewpro.com
- JobInterview.net   www.job-interview.net
- Interview Coach   www.interviewcoach.com
- Quintessential Careers   www.quintcareers.com/
                                 intvres.html
- Wetfeet.com   www.wetfeet.com/advice/
                                 interviewing.asp
- The Riley Guide   www.rileyguide.com/
                                 interview.html
- Jobweb   www.jobweb.com/Resumes_
                                 Interviews/default.htm
- WinningTheJob   www.winningthejob.com
- WSACorp.com   www.WSACorp.com

In preparation for the critical salary negotiation session, which is an extension of the job interview (should only occur after you have been offered the job), we recommend the following resources:

Books

101 Salary Secrets (Daniel Porot)
The $100,000+ Job Interview (Wendy S. Enelow)
Are You Paid What You're Worth? (Michael F. O'Malley and Suzanne Oaks)
Better Than Money (David E. Gumpert)
Dynamite Salary Negotiations (Ron and Caryl Krannich)
Get More Money On Your Next Job (Lee E. Miller)
Get Paid What You're Worth (Robin Pinkley and Gregory Northcraft)
Get a Raise in 7 Days (Ron and Caryl Krannich)
Haldane's Best Salary Tips for Professionals (Bernard Haldane Associates)
Interviewing and Salary Negotiation (Kate Wendleton)

Negotiating Your Salary (Jack Chapman)
Perks and Parachutes (Paul Fargis)
Rites of Passage at $100,000 to $1 Million+ (John Lucht)
*Smart Woman's Guide to Interviewing and Salary
    Negotiations* (Julie Adair King)

Websites

- Salary.com   www.salary.com
- JobStar   www.jobstar.org
- Monster.com   http://salary.monster.com
- SalaryExpert.com   www.salaryexpert.com
- SalarySource   www.salarysource.com
- WageWeb.com   www.wageweb.com
- Abbott-Langer   www.abbott-langer. com
- BenefitsLink.com   www.benefitslink.com
- BenefitNews.com   www.benefitnews.com
- Bureau of Labor Statistics   www.bls.gov
- CareerJournal   www.careerjournal.com
- CompGeo Online   www.claytonwallis.com/
                                 cxgonl.html

- Employee Benefit
  Research Institute   www.ebri.org
- Homestore.com   www.homefair.com
- Quintessential Careers   www.quintcareers.com/
                                 salary_negotiation.html

- Riley Guide   www.rileyguide.com/
                                 netintv.html

- Robert Half International   www.rhii.com
- Salary Surveys for   www.salarysurveys.
  Northwest Employers   milliman.com

Be Honest But Not Stupid

Honesty is always the best policy when conducting a job search as well as doing the job. However, more and more job seekers cut corners and misrepresent themselves on resumes and in interviews.

Let's take an ethics quiz on the job search. Respond to the following statements by indicating your degree of agreement with each:

The Ethics Quiz

SCALE: 1 = strongly agree   4 = disagree
             2 = agree   5 = strongly disagree
             3 = maybe, not certain

1. Honesty is always the best policy
    when conducting a job search.   1   2   3   4   5

2. Honest people finish last in today's
    competitive job market.   1   2   3   4   5

3. Employers prefer hiring frank and
    honest people who always tell the
    truth, including the whole truth.   1   2   3   4   5

4. Employers are no more honest about
    themselves than candidates. Everyone
    exaggerates on their resume.   1   2   3   4   5

5. I should be up-front and tell employers
    early on what I really want – more
    money and better health benefits.   1   2   3   4   5

6. I'll give the employer what he wants –
    a story of someone (me) who he thinks
    can walk on water.   1   2   3   4   5

7. If true, I should indicate on my resume
    or in my cover letter that I was fired
    from my last job.   1   2   3   4   5

8. It's none of the employer's business that
    I was fired. If asked, I'll tell her that I left
    because of a dishonest boss who was likely
    to go to jail!   1   2   3   4   5

9. When asked why I didn't complete school
    I should tell the truth about my problems
    with drugs and alcohol.   1   2   3   4   5

10. When asked why I didn't complete
    school, I'll make up a story about my
    dying mother or a career opportunity
    I couldn't pass up.   1   2   3   4   5

11. I should let the employer know that I'm
a single mother trying to support three
small children.   1 2 3 4 5

12. I'll tell the employer I have a great
family life.   1 2 3 4 5

13. When asked to explain why I have a
two-year employment gap, I should
be honest and tell the employer about
my incarceration for drug dealing. But
I'm clean now.   1 2 3 4 5

14. When asked to explain why I have a
two-year employment gap, I'll tell
the employer I needed to take some
time off to reassess my career goals.   1 2 3 4 5

15. If true, I should tell the employer that
I have a bipolar disorder but that I have
this illness under control with medication.   1 2 3 4 5

16. If an employer asks any mental health
questions, I'll try to remain calm and
remind him that he's asking a totally
inappropriate question.   1 2 3 4 5

17. I should tell the interviewer that I'm
pregnant and that I'll need six weeks of
maternity leave in another six months.   1 2 3 4 5

18. I'll wait until I'm on the job a few weeks
before telling the employer I need six weeks
maternity leave starting in September.   1 2 3 4 5

If you agree or strongly agreed with the odd-numbered statements, you have a propensity to be honest but stupid in the job search. On the other hand, if you agreed or strongly agreed with the even-numbered statements, you verge on being dishonest but "smart." If you're somewhere in the middle on all of the statements, you may not be making this type of mistake. Let's elaborate on what we mean by honest but stupid and dishonest but smart job seekers.

There's no rule that says you must confess your sins and volunteer negative information about yourself in the job search. That would be stupid since it might knock you out of consideration for no good reason other than your own self-destruction. Take, for example, these two contrasting statements from two candidates who left their last jobs for the same reason. They tell the truth two different ways:

I didn't get along with my boss.

I thought it was time to move on to more challenging opportunities.

Both statements are 100 percent honest, but the first one is naive and stupid. It labels the person as someone who may have difficulty handling authority and who personalizes workplace issues. The second statement is honest and professional. It emphasizes that the candidate may have professional goals and a larger vision of where she wants to go career-wise. If given a choice, employers would shy away from hiring the first candidate. The second candidate has what employers desire – honesty, professionalism, and tact.

While employers definitely want honest and sincere employees, they are not particularly attracted to brutally frank employees who mistake their frankness for honesty. Indeed, some of the most honest people say the stupidest things about themselves to others. They confess their sins, volunteer negative information about themselves, and reveal personal details that make others uncomfortable. Indeed, they may become living soap operas with revealing tales of their many struggles to survive and prosper against so many odds. Such frankness is inappropriate in a job search. It sets you up for failure by accurately labeling you for what you really are – honest but stupid. Employers cannot afford to hire such people.

Employers want you to be truthful about your education, training, skills, and accomplishments as they relate to the job and workplace. They are not really interested in getting involved in the trials and tribulations of your personal life, however interesting it may be to you. Those are inappropriate and uncomfortable subjects for employers. Don't bore them with the details of your marriage, family, health, religion, politics, and travel.

Employers seem to increasingly encounter dishonest but "smart" candidates who deliberately lie on their resumes and in interviews. Indeed, recent studies conducted on verifying claims on resumes have indicated that over 50 percent of job seekers lie on their resumes, from educational credentials to job titles, employers, and employment dates. Many candidates feel compelled to make up dishonest or deceptive stories in order to get the interview and job offer.

Too many employers have been burnt by such candidates to rely only on the resume and interviews for making hiring decisions. Except for very small companies that often neglect to do their screening homework, more and more employers are hiring smarter as they increasingly use outside groups to verify credentials, ask more probing questions of references, and subject candidates to testing, including psychological profiles and polygraphs. The days of dishonest but smart job seekers may be numbered, especially with employers who do their homework in screening candidates.

Dishonest but "smart" job seekers should be forewarned that there is a high probability of catching their deception in today's security-conscious job market. Many employers simply expect to be lied to by candidates. They will check you out. If not, they will probably discover your pattern of deception once you're on the job. Indeed, dishonest but "smart" job seekers have a habit of making revealing mistakes on the job.

Commit Yourself to Implementation

Implementation will be the key to your successful job search. You can dream and plan all you want, but if you don't have a plan of action that takes you through the seven-step job search process, those dreams and plans will go nowhere. In fact, they may frustrate and possibly depress you since you will be setting yourself up for failure by not implementing.

Time and again we find successful job hunters are the ones who routinize specific job search activities. They make contact after contact, conduct numerous informational interviews, submit many applications and resumes, and keep repeating these activities in spite of encountering rejections. They learn that success is just a few more *"no's"* and informational interviews away. They face each day with a positive attitude fit for someone desiring to change their life – I must collect my ten *"no's"* today because each *"no"* brings me closer to another *"yes"*!

You may find it useful to commit yourself in writing to achieving job search success. This is a very useful way to get both motivated and directed for action. Start by completing the job search contract on page

191 and keep it near you – in your briefcase or on your desk.

In addition, you should complete weekly performance reports. These reports identify what you actually accomplished rather than what your good intentions tell you to do. Make copies of the performance and planning report form on page 192 and use one each week to track your actual progress and to plan your activities for the next week.

If you fail to meet these written commitments, issue yourself a revised and updated contract. But if you do this three or more times, we strongly suggest you stop kidding yourself about your motivation and commitment to find a job. Start over again, but this time consult a professional career counselor who can assist you with your job search. A professional may not be cheap, but if paying for help gets you on the right track and results in the job you want, it's money well spent. Do not be *"penny wise but pound foolish"* with your future. If you must seek professional advice, be sure you are an informed consumer according to our advice on "shopping for a professional" in Chapter 3.

Job Search Contract

1. I'm committed to changing my life by changing my job. Today's date is _____.

2. I will manage my time so that I can successfully complete my job search and find a high quality job. I will begin changing my time management behavior on _____.

3. I will begin my job search on _____.

4. I will involve _____ with my job search.
   (individual/group)

5. I will spend at least one week conducting library and Internet research on different jobs, employers, and organizations. I will begin this research during the week of _____.

6. I will complete my skills identification step by _____.

7. I will complete my objective statement by _____.

8. I will complete my resume by _____.

9. Each week I will:

   ■ make _____ new job contacts.

   ■ conduct _____ informational interviews.

   ■ follow up on _____ referrals.

10. My first job interview will take place during the week of _____.

11. I will begin my new job by _____.

12. I will make a habit of learning one new skill each year.

Signature: _____

Date: _____

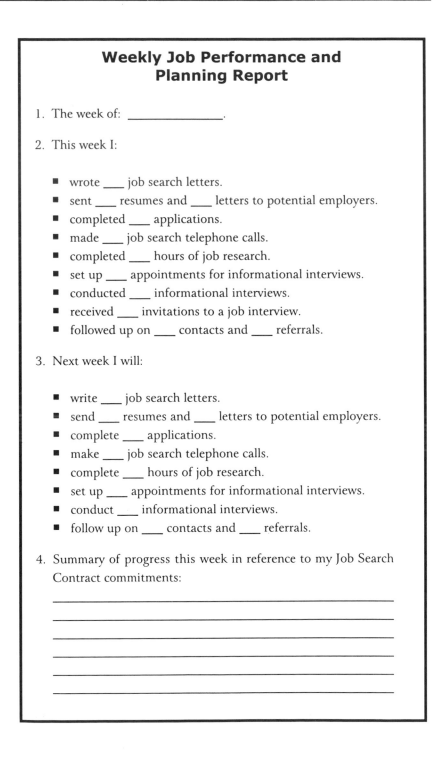

Weekly Job Performance and Planning Report

1. The week of: _____.

2. This week I:

   - wrote ____ job search letters.
   - sent ____ resumes and ____ letters to potential employers.
   - completed ____ applications.
   - made ____ job search telephone calls.
   - completed ____ hours of job research.
   - set up ____ appointments for informational interviews.
   - conducted ____ informational interviews.
   - received ____ invitations to a job interview.
   - followed up on ____ contacts and ____ referrals.

3. Next week I will:

   - write ____ job search letters.
   - send ____ resumes and ____ letters to potential employers.
   - complete ____ applications.
   - make ____ job search telephone calls.
   - complete ____ hours of job research.
   - set up ____ appointments for informational interviews.
   - conduct ____ informational interviews.
   - follow up on ____ contacts and ____ referrals.

4. Summary of progress this week in reference to my Job Search Contract commitments:

   _____
   _____
   _____
   _____
   _____
   _____

Index

193

The Authors

FOR MORE THAN TWO DECADES Ron and Caryl Krannich have pursued a passion – assisting hundreds of thousands of individuals, from students, the unemployed, and ex-offenders to military personnel, international job seekers, and CEOs, in making critical job and career transitions. Focusing on key job search skills, career changes, and employment fields, their impressive body of work has helped shape career thinking and behavior both in the United States and abroad. Their sound advice has changed numerous lives, including their own!

Ron and Caryl are two of America's leading career and travel writers who have authored, co-authored, or ghost-written more than 70 books. A former Peace Corps Volunteer and Fulbright Scholar, Ron received his Ph.D. in Political Science from Northern Illinois University. Caryl received her Ph.D. in Speech Communication from Penn State University. Together they operate Development Concepts Incorporated, a training, consulting, and publishing firm in Virginia.

The Krannichs are both former university professors, high school teachers, management trainers, and consultants. As trainers and consultants, they have completed numerous projects on management, career development, local government, population planning, and rural development in the United States and abroad. Their career books focus on key job search skills, military and civilian career transitions, government and international careers, travel jobs, and nonprofit organizations, and include such classics as ***High Impact Resumes and Letters***, ***Interview for Success***, and ***Change Your Job, Change Your Life***. Their books represent one of today's most comprehensive collections of career writing. With nearly 3 million copies in print, their publications are widely available in bookstores, libraries, and career centers. No strangers to the Internet world, they have written ***America's Top Internet Job Sites*** and ***The Directory of Websites for International Jobs*** and published several Internet recruitment and job search books. They also have developed career-related websites: www.impactpublications.com, www.winningthejob.com, www.contentfor careers.com, and www.veteransworld.com. Many of their career tips have appeared on such major websites as www.monster.com, www.careerbuild er.com, www.employmentguide.com, and www.campuscareercenter.com.

Ron and Caryl live a double life, with travel being their best kept *"do what you love"* career secret. Authors of over 20 travel-shopping guidebooks on various destinations around the world, they continue to pursue their international and travel interests through their innovative ***Treasures and Pleasures of...Best of the Best*** travel-shopping series and related websites: www.ishoparoundtheworld.com, www.contentfortravel.com, and www.tra vel-smarter.com. When not found at their home and business in Virginia, they are probably somewhere in Europe, Asia, Africa, the Middle East, the South Pacific, the Caribbean, or the Americas following their other passion – researching and writing about quality antiques, arts, crafts, jewelry, hotels, and restaurants as well as adhering to the career advice they give to others: *"Pursue a passion that enables you to do what you really love to do."*

As both career and travel experts, the Krannichs' work is frequently featured in major newspapers, magazines, and newsletters as well as on radio, television, and the Internet. Available for interviews, consultation, and presentations, they can be contacted as follows:

Ron and Caryl Krannich
krannich@impactpublications.com

Career Resources

T HE FOLLOWING CAREER RESOURCES are available directly from Impact Publications. Full descriptions of each title as well as downloadable catalogs, specialty fliers, posters, videos, and software can be found at www.impactpublications.com. Complete the following form or list the titles, include shipping (see formula at the end), enclose payment, and send your order to:

IMPACT PUBLICATIONS
9104 Manassas Drive, Suite N
Manassas Park, VA 20111-5211 USA
1-800-361-1055 (orders only)
Tel. 703-361-7300 or Fax 703-335-9486
Email address: info@impactpublications.com
Quick & easy online ordering: www.impactpublications.com

Orders from individuals must be prepaid by check, money order, or major credit card. We accept telephone, fax, and email orders.

Qty.	TITLES	Price	TOTAL
Featured Title			
____	I Want to Do Something Else, But I'm Not Sure What It Is	$15.95	_____
Other Titles By Authors			
____	101 Secrets of Highly Effective Speakers	$15.95	_____
____	201 Dynamite Job Search Letters	$19.95	_____
____	America's Top Internet Job Sites	$19.95	_____
____	America's Top 100 Jobs for People Re-Entering the Workforce	$19.95	_____
____	America's Top 100 Jobs for People Without a Four-Year Degree	$19.95	_____
____	Change Your Job, Change Your Life	$21.95	_____
____	Discover the Best Jobs for You	$15.95	_____
____	Dynamite Salary Negotiations	$15.95	_____

_____ The Ex-Offender's Job Hunting Guide	$14.95	_____
_____ High Impact Resumes and Letters	$19.95	_____
_____ Interview for Success	$15.95	_____
_____ The Job Hunting Guide	$14.95	_____
_____ Job Hunting Tips for People With Not-So-Hot Backgrounds	$17.95	_____
_____ Job Interview Tips for People With Not-So-Hot Backgrounds	$14.95	_____
_____ Military Resumes and Cover Letters	$21.95	_____
_____ Nail the Cover Letter!	$17.95	_____
_____ Nail the Job Interview!	$13.95	_____
_____ Nail the Resume!	$17.95	_____
_____ No One Will Hire Me!	$13.95	_____
_____ Savvy Interviewing: The Nonverbal Advantage	$10.95	_____
_____ The Savvy Networker	$13.95	_____
_____ The Savvy Resume Writer	$12.95	_____

Testing and Assessment

_____ Career Tests	$12.95	_____
_____ Discover What You're Best At	$14.00	_____
_____ Do What You Are	$18.95	_____
_____ Finding Your Perfect Work	$16.95	_____
_____ I Could Do Anything If Only I Knew What It Was	$14.95	_____
_____ I Don't Know What I Want, But I Know It's Not This	$14.00	_____
_____ Now, Discover Your Strengths	$27.00	_____
_____ Quit Your Job and Grow Some Hair	$15.95	_____
_____ What Color Is Your Parachute?	$17.95	_____
_____ What Should I Do With My Life?	$14.95	_____
_____ What Type Am I?	$14.95	_____
_____ What's Your Type of Career?	$17.95	_____

Inspiration and Empowerment

_____ 7 Habits of Highly Effective People (2nd Edition)	$15.00	_____
_____ The 8th Habit: From Effectiveness to Greatness	$26.00	_____
_____ 100 Ways to Motivate Yourself	$14.99	_____
_____ Attitude Is Everything	$14.95	_____
_____ Do What You Love for the Rest of Your Life	$24.95	_____
_____ Dream It Do It	$16.95	_____
_____ How to Create Your Own Luck	$24.95	_____
_____ Life Strategies	$13.95	_____
_____ Luck Is No Accident: Making the Most of Happenstance	$15.95	_____
_____ Practical Dreamer's Handbook	$13.95	_____
_____ The Purpose-Driven Life	$19.99	_____
_____ Self Matters	$13.95	_____
_____ Who Moved My Cheese?	$19.95	_____

Resumes and Letters

_____ 101 Great Tips for a Dynamite Resume	$13.95	_____
_____ Best KeyWords for Resumes, Cover Letters, & Interviews	$17.95	_____
_____ Best Resumes and CVs for International Jobs	$24.95	_____
_____ Best Resumes for $100,000+ Jobs	$24.95	_____
_____ Best Resumes for People Without a Four-Year Degree	$19.95	_____

_____	Best Cover Letters for $100,000+ Jobs	$24.95 _____
_____	Cover Letters for Dummies	$16.99 _____
_____	Expert Resumes for People Returning to Work	$16.95 _____
_____	Haldane's Best Cover Letters for Professionals	$15.95 _____
_____	Haldane's Best Resumes for Professionals	$15.95 _____
_____	Resumes for Dummies	$16.99 _____

Networking, Dress, Interviews, Salary Negotiations

_____	The $100,000+ Job Interview	$19.95 _____
_____	Dressing Smart for Men	$16.95 _____
_____	Dressing Smart for Women	$16.95 _____
_____	A Foot in the Door	$14.95 _____
_____	Haldane's Best Answers to Tough Interview Questions	$15.95 _____
_____	Haldane's Best Salary Tips for Professionals	$15.95 _____
_____	KeyWords to Nail Your Job Interview	$17.95 _____
_____	Masters of Networking	$16.95 _____
_____	Networking for Job Search and Career Success	$16.95 _____

SUBTOTAL   _____

Virginia residents add 5% sales tax   _____

POSTAGE/HANDLING ($5 for first
product and 8% of SUBTOTAL) $5.00

8% of SUBTOTAL --   _____

TOTAL ENCLOSED ----------------------------------   _____

SHIP TO:

NAME _____

ADDRESS: _____

_____

_____

PAYMENT METHOD:

❑   I enclose check/money order for $ _____ made payable to
    IMPACT PUBLICATIONS.

❑   Please charge $ _____ to my credit card:

    ❑ Visa   ❑ MasterCard   ❑ American Express   ❑ Discover

    Card # _____ Expiration date: / ___

    Signature _____

Keep in Touch . . .
On the Web!

www.impactpublications.com
www.ishoparoundtheworld.com
www.travel-smarter.com
www.contentfortravel.com
www.winningthejob.com
www.veteransworld.com
www.contentforcareers.com